YONDE KAITE

よんでかいて

JAPANESE WORKBOOK

PRIMARY LEVEL 5

WRITTEN BY

ANNE RAJAKUMAR

WITH ORIGINAL ILLUSTRATIONS BY

JENNIFER CHENG

First published in 1999, reprinted in 2001, 2011, 2014
This redesigned edition first published in 2017

Insight Publications Pty Ltd
3/350 Charman Road
Cheltenham Victoria 3192
Australia

Tel: +61 3 8571 4950
Fax: +61 3 8571 0257
Email: books@insightpublications.com.au

www.insightpublications.com.au

ISBN: 9781875882496

Illustrations by Jennifer Cheng; other images courtesy of Shutterstock
Cover and internal design by Gisela Beer
Proofing by Sage Napthine-Morrison and Fabrice Wilmann

Printed by Markono Print Media Pte Ltd

Author acknowledgements
Special thanks to my family, Kumar, Timothy and Jessica, for their constant support and assistance and to Barbara and Chris for their untiring advice and unwavering encouragement and help.

TABLE OF CONTENTS

LANGUAGE AND EXTENSION LESSONS

WRITING AND EXTENSION LESSONS

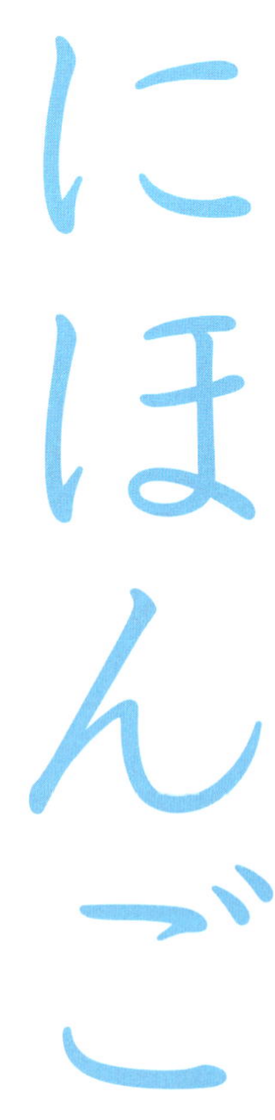
にほんご

♂ – boy
♀ – girl

name + さん / you ♀ / name + くん / you ♂	は (particle WA)

なに	じん	です	か
what	person (nationality)	are	?

わたし / I ♀ / ぼく / I ♂	は (particle WA)			です (am)
		にほん じん	Japanese	
		ちゅうごく じん	Chinese	
		オーストラリア じん	Australian	
		ニュージーランド じん	New Zealander	
		アメリカ じん	American	
		カナダ じん	Canadian	
		イギリス じん	English	
		ロシア じん	Russian	

Draw the children's faces in the boxes where they belong.

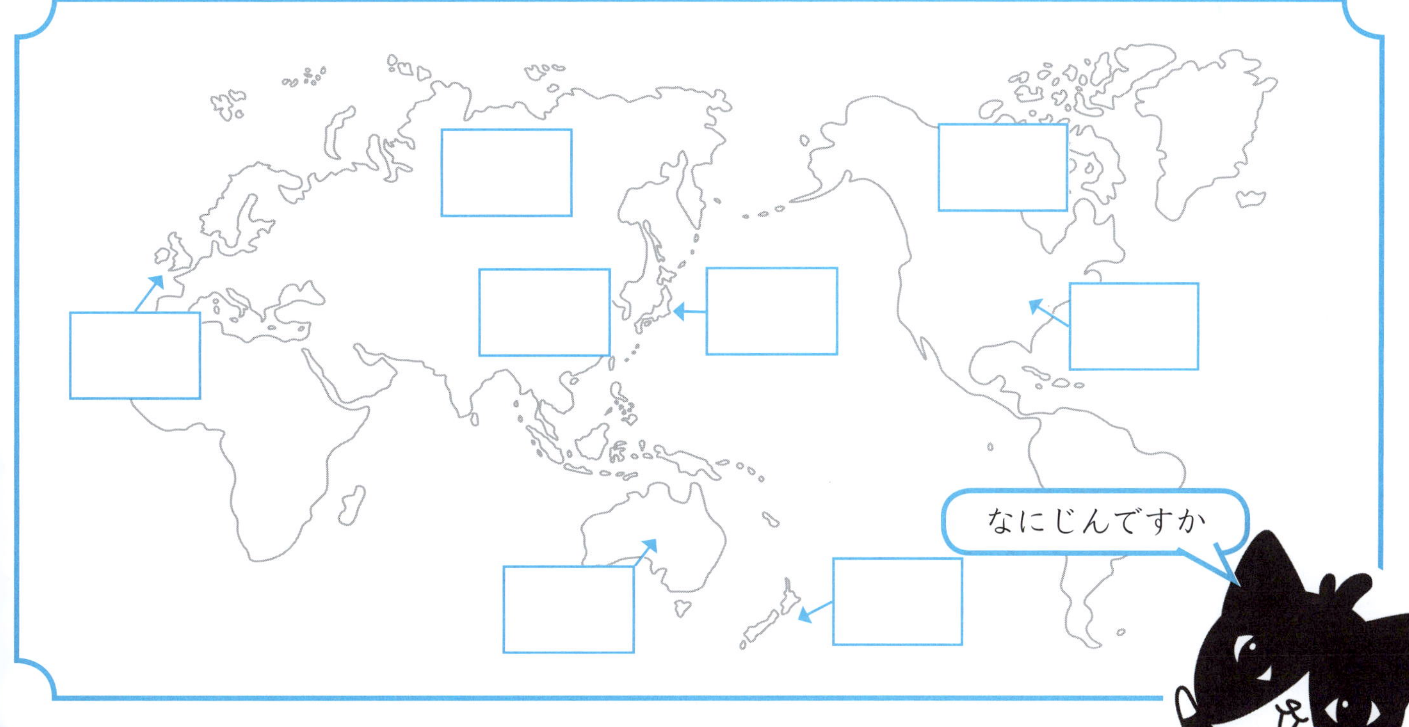

 イギリスじん

 アメリカじん

 オーストラリアじん

 ちゅうごくじん

 ロシアじん

 カナダじん

 ニュージーランドじん

 にほんじん

Write the following sentences/phrases in Japanese to find the mystery nationality. Use the wordlist at the back of the book if you need to.

1. Where do you live?
2. I like books.
3. Hello / Good day!
4. two o'clock
5. I like Japan.

Read the letters downwards to find the mystery nationality.

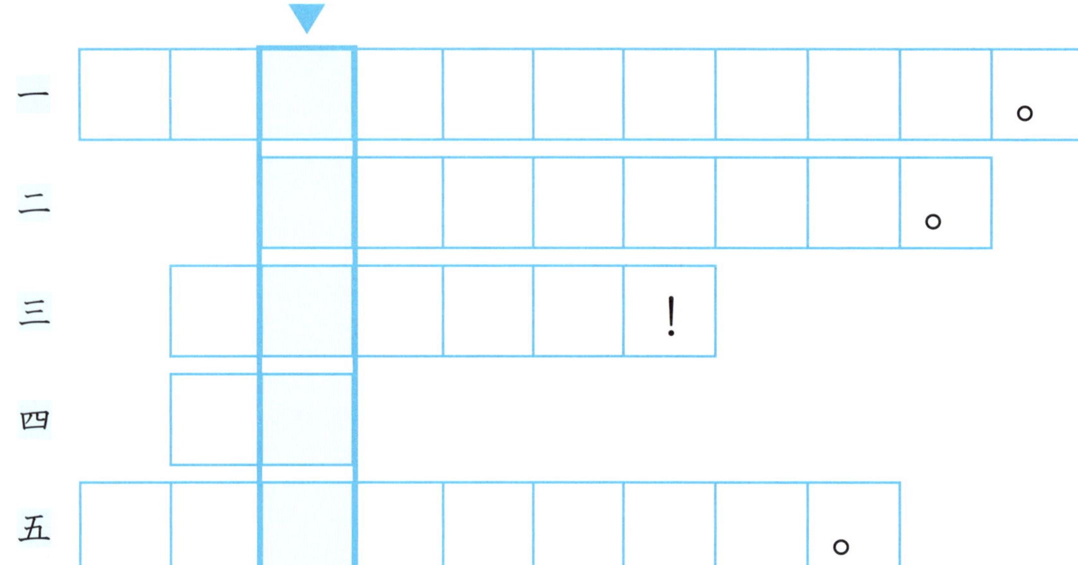

The mystery nationality is:

Japanese	English

Fill in the missing hiragana/katakana letters to complete these nationalities.

一 Australian ☐ ース ☐ ラリ ☐ じん

二 New Zealander ニュ ☐ ジ ☐ ラ ☐ ド ☐ ん

三 Canadian ☐ ナ ☐☐ ん

四 American ☐ メ ☐☐ じ ☐

五 Japanese ☐ ほ ☐ じん

しゅみ	は	なん	です	か
hobby	particle WA	what	is	?

わたし の
my♀
ぼく の
my♂

しゅみ	は	スポーツ	sport	です
		おんがく	music	
		どくしょ	reading	
hobby	particle WA	コンピュータゲーム	computer games	is
		ショッピング	shopping	

Look at the pictures to help you write a dialogue for each pair of children. The first one has been done for you to trace over.

Use the vocabulary boxes at the top of previous pages and the wordlist at the back of the book to help you read the following self introduction, then answer the questions in English or Japanese.

はじめまして。わたしのなまえは、はなです。
十一さいです。五ねんせいです。とうきょうにすんでいます。
ほんがすきです。わたしのしゅみは、どくしょです。どうぞよろしく。

一　このひとのなまえは、なんですか。

____

二　このひとは、なんさいですか。

____

三　このひとは、なんねんせいですか。

____

四　このひとは、どこにすんでいますか。

____

五　このひとは、なにがすきですか。

____

六　このひとのしゅみは、なんですか。

____

このひと
= this person

このひとの
= this person's

Can you remember the colour, clothes and body words?
Colour the picture of Taka (たか) according to the information below. Look up any words you need to at the back of the book.

たかくんの = Taka's

たかくんのシャツは、あかです。
たかくんのズボンは、あおです。
たかくんのくつしたは、みどりです。
たかくんのくつは、きいろです。
たかくんのかみのけは、ちゃいろです。
たかくんのめは、くろです。

はじめまして。	I'm pleased to meet you.

わたし の my ♀	なまえ name	は particle WA	☺ name ☺	です is
ぼく の my ♂	しゅみ hobby		スポーツ sport	

わたし I ♀	は particle WA	☺ age ☺ さい	です am
ぼく I ♂		☺ grade ☺ ねんせい	
		☺ country ☺ じん	

☺ place ☺ に すんでいます。	I live in ☺ place ☺.

どうぞよろしく おねがいします。	a formal greeting used after self introduction

Pipi has brought a friend of his along to school and the teacher has asked the new student to introduce himself/herself to the class in Japanese. Fortunately, Pipi's friend is very good at Japanese. Draw a picture of the friend and write what you think he/she might have said in the speech bubble. Make up the details yourself! Use one box for each letter (the same rule applies when using roomaji letters). It is okay to break a word to go on to the next line. If you want to make a list, use the Japanese word for 'and' – と.

Look at the clues in the pictures of the two children below, then write a self introduction for each of them. Guess any information that you cannot find in the pictures.

Can you write the following words/phrases in Japanese without looking them up?

一 I'm pleased to meet you.

二 grade 5

三 my (used by girls)

四 my (used by boys)

五 hobby

六 music

はじめまして。	I'm pleased to meet you.
おげんき ですか。	How are you? (Are you well?)
(はい) げんき です。	I'm fine. (Yes, I'm well.)

わたし の my ♀	なまえ name	は	☺ name ☺	です
ぼく の my ♂	しゅみ hobby	particle WA	スポーツ sport	is

わたし I ♀	は	☺ age ☺ さい	です
ぼく I ♂	particle WA	☺ grade ☺ ねんせい ☺ country ☺ じん	am

☺ place ☺ に すんでいます。	I live in ☺ place ☺.

どうぞよろしく おねがいします。	a formal greeting used after self introduction

Pipi is going on a trip to Japan, where he will be staying with a Japanese host family, the Kumamotos. He has written a letter to his host family introducing himself. Read the letter and answer the questions below. Answer the questions in English or Japanese. Choose Japanese if you can!

☺name☺ へ = To ☺name☺
☺name☺ より = From ☺name☺
When we use へ in this way, we pronounce it like an え.

くまもとさんへ

はじめまして。おげんきですか。ぼくのなまえは、ピピです。
十一さいです。オーストラリアじんです。シドニーにすんでいます。
五ねんせいです。ぼくのたんじょうびは、六がつです。しゅみは、
スポーツです。どうぞよろしくおねがいします。

ピピより

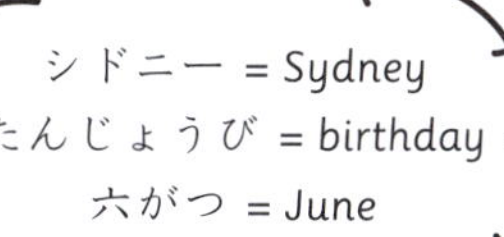

一 Where does Pipi live? ______________________

二 How old is Pipi? ______________________

三 What grade is Pipi in? ______________________

四 When is Pipi's birthday? ______________________

五 What is Pipi's hobby? ______________________

六 How do you write Pipi using katakana letters? ______________________

Pipi has decided that he wants to make a very good impression with his self-introduction letter, so he has decided to rewrite his letter in the traditional Japanese way, writing vertically instead of horizontally, and starting from the right-hand side of the page. Look carefully at the changes he has made.

くまもとさんへ

　はじめまして。おげ
んきですか。ぼくのな
まえは、ピピです。十
一さいです。オースト
ラリアじんです。シド
ニーにすんでいます。
五ねんせいです。ぼく
のたんじょうびは、六
がつです。しゅみは、
スポーツです。どうぞ
よろしくおねがいしま
す。

　　　　　　ピピより

Try writing your own letter in the same way.

わたし I♀ ぼく I♂	は
name + さん name♀ name + くん name♂	particle WA

スポーツ	sport
おんがく	music
どくしょ	reading
コンピュータゲーム	computer games
ショッピング	shopping

... が すき です。 I like ...
... が だいすき です。 I love ...
... は、あまり すきじゃない です。 I don't really like ...

Look at each sentence carefully, then use it to make a picture sentence. A picture sentence is a picture with a sentence included in it. The first one has been done for you, as an example.

おんがくが
だいすきです。

どくしょが
すきです。

コンピュータゲームは、
あまり
すきじゃないです。

Find and shade, in different colours, the words and sentences listed below the word search. Write them into the table in Japanese. Look for words down, across and diagonally.

い	ぱ	わ	は	き	ど	が	ぺ	あ	に	ほ	ん	じ	ん	む	ね
ゅ	ば	た	も	あ	ち	ゅ	う	ご	く	じ	ん	か	ぷ	カ	へ
ひ	う	し	な	と	め	ぴ	え	な	ぼ	お	ほ	で	み	ナ	ぬ
ど	や	の	ゃ	し	ゅ	み	は	な	ん	で	す	か	に	ダ	ま
く	三	な	ろ	べ	ぎ	び	二	く	の	ふ	す	五	ぶ	じ	ぽ
し	わ	ま	ろ	ぜ	せ	い	っ	ず	九	で	あ	八	そ	ん	た
ょ	づ	え	お	ん	が	く	る	よ	き	ん	ご	ち	し	で	ゆ
う	の	は	じ	め	ま	し	て	ん	を	す	だ	ょ	そ	す	ち
に	し	ゅ	つ	じ	さ	れ	げ	た	ぼ	五	ね	ん	せ	い	ぐ
ぎ	よ	じ	ど	ざ	さ	お	か	こ	げ	え	ぷ	く	け	ぷ	ぞ

Look for these English words and phrases:	Write them in Japanese here:						
music							
reading							
Japanese (person)							
grade 5							
my name (used by girls)							
I'm pleased to meet you.							
Chinese (person)							

Look for these English sentences:	Write them in Japanese here:										
What's your hobby?											
How are you?											
I'm Canadian.											

わたし	は
I♀	
ぼく	
I♂	
name + さん	
name♀	
name + くん	particle WA
name♂	
おかあさん	
mother	
おとうさん	
father	

どんな スポーツ を します か。	What kind of sport do you play?

スポーツ	sport	を	します
サッカー	soccer		
クリケット	cricket		
フットボール	football		
テニス	tennis		
バスケットボール	basketball	particle O	play/do
すいえい	swimming		
やきゅう	baseball		
じゅうどう	judo		

Look at the sentences about Taka and his mother below, then fill in the blank boxes to make the Japanese sentences match the English sentences. The first one has been done for you to trace over.

Taka likes baseball.

たか [く][ん] は、やきゅう [が] すき [で][す]。

Taka plays baseball.

[ ][ ] くんは、[ ][ ][ ][ ] をします。

Mother's hobby is tennis.

おかあさんの [ ][ ][ ] は、テニス [ ][ ]。

Mother plays tennis.

[ ][ ][ ][ ][ ] は、[ ][ ][ ] をします。

Now complete the sentences below so that they are true for you, then draw a matching picture.

What kind of sport do you play?

[ ][ ][ ] スポーツ [ ] しますか。

I play ________________.

[ ][ ][ ][ ][ ][ ][ ][ ][ ][ ][ ][ ][ ][ ][ ][ ][ ][ ]

Read the story about Mei Lin （メイ・リン）, then look at the statements about her in the box below. Collect the hiragana letter clues in brackets after each **correct** statement and ignore the hiragana letter clues if the statement is **incorrect**. Unjumble the letter clues that you have collected to find the name of a popular Japanese cartoon.

About Mei Lin:

メイ・リンさんは、十二さいです。六ねんせいです。
ちゅうごくじんです。
メイ・リンさんのしゅみは、スポーツです。
メイ・リンさんは、テニスとすいえいをします。
べんきょうは、あまりすきじゃないです。

Here are some true and false statements about Mei Lin. Collect the letter clues after the true statements.

メイ・リンさんは、十二さいです。（も）
メイ・リンさんは、十二ねんせいです。（ふ）
メイ・リンさんは、ちゅうごくじんです。（ん）
メイ・リンさんは、じゅうどうとすいえいをします。（き）
メイ・リンさんは、べんきょうがすきです。（の）
メイ・リンさんは、テニスとすいえいをします。（ぽ）
メイ・リンさんのしゅみは、スポーツです。（け）

The hiragana letter clues: | | | | |

The name of the Japanese cartoon (in Japanese): | | | | |

The name of the Japanese cartoon (in English): ____

Read the sentences below and work out what is wrong with each one. Rewrite the sentences so that they make sense.

一　ぼくは、Rebecca です。

______

二　わたしのしゅみは、六さいです。

______

三　すいえいにすんでいます。

______

わたし I♀	は
ぼく I♂	
name + さん name♀	
name + くん name♂	particle WA
おかあさん mother	
おとうさん father	

スポーツ	sport	を
サッカー	soccer	
クリケット	cricket	
フットボール	football	
テニス	tennis	
バスケットボール	basketball	particle O
すいえい	swimming	
やきゅう	baseball	
じゅうどう	judo	

しますか Do (you) play/do?
します (I) play/do
しません (I) don't play/do

Look at the vocabulary boxes above and work out how you would ask someone if they play a certain sport. Write your Japanese question next to the English version of the question.

Do you play football? ____________________

Do you swim? ____________________

Now, think about how you would answer these questions. Write your Japanese answer next to the English version of the answer.

Yes, I play football. はい、____________________

No, I don't play football. いいえ、____________________

Now use these sentence patterns to conduct a class survey and complete the sports table below. Ask at least ten people in your class if they play the sports you have included in your table. Write the sports you wish to ask about along the bottom of the table, and colour in one box above that sport for each person who plays it.

NUMBER OF STUDENTS							
	十一						
	十						
	九						
	八						
	七						
	六						
	五						
	四						
	三						
	二						
	一						
SPORT ▶							

Put the Japanese words and particles in the correct order to make complete sentences, then translate the sentences into English. Use the wordlist at the back of the book if you need it.

Japanese words	は　にほん　じん　です　ぼく
Japanese sentence	
English sentence	

Japanese words	しゅみ　は　どくしょ　わたし　です　の
Japanese sentence	
English sentence	

Japanese words	じゅうどう　すきじゃない　です　あまり　は
Japanese sentence	
English sentence	

Now try unjumbling each Japanese word before putting them in the correct order to make complete sentences!

Japanese words	くぼ　を　どゅじうう　せしんま　は
Japanese sentence	
English sentence	

Japanese words	とおんさう　は　みゅし　の　すで　テスニ
Japanese sentence	
English sentence	

Japanese words	きがすすで　いすいえ　は　たわし
Japanese sentence	
English sentence	

Japanese words	いだきすが　すで　んがおく
Japanese sentence	
English sentence	

いつ	when

げつようび	Monday	に
かようび	Tuesday	
すいようび	Wednesday	
もくようび	Thursday	
きんようび	Friday	on
どようび	Saturday	
にちようび	Sunday	

スポーツ	sport	を
サッカー	soccer	
クリケット	cricket	
フットボール	football	
テニス	tennis	
バスケットボール	basketball	particle o
すいえい	swimming	
やきゅう	baseball	
じゅうどう	judo	

しますか
Do (you) play/do?
します
(I) play/do
しません
(I) don't play/do

If you want to specify who the topic of your sentence is (i.e. the person the sentence is about), put the person's name or description (e.g. Jack or おかあさん) at the beginning of the sentence, followed by topic particle は. If the sentence is about yourself, you may include ぼく (I – used by boys) or わたし (I – used by girls) followed by topic pacticle は, although you do not need to.

Pipi likes playing sport very much. Look at his busy schedule, then answer the questions below. The first one has been done for you to trace over. If you have time, write 'I like sport' in Japanese in Pipi's speech bubble. Notice that Pipi's name is followed by chan (ちゃん). This is often used after the names of young children, girls and small animals – instead of san (さん) or kun (くん) – by people who are close to them.

げつようび	かようび	すいようび	もくようび	きんようび	どようび	にちようび
テニス	バスケットボール	すいえい	やきゅう テニス	じゅうどう	サッカー テニス	フットボール

一 ピピちゃんは、いつバスケットボールをしますか。

ピピちゃんは、かようびにバスケットボールをします。

二 ピピちゃんは、いつフットボールをしますか。

三 ピピちゃんは、もくようびにやきゅうをしますか。

四 ピピちゃんは、クリケットをしますか。

Complete the following table by writing one Japanese sentence for each day of the week. You must include the day of the week in your sentence, but the rest is up to your imagination. Try to use as many different sentence patterns as you can.

げつようび	
かようび	
すいようび	
もくようび	
きんようび	
どようび	
にちようび	

Connect the following letters with lines to makes words or phrases. List the words/ phrases that you make below.

ぼ しゅ く よ ま に す お ん い さ

み ど お の な が び え え や

う く

す し げ を が い う きゅ 十

き ま ん に ほ す ん き で す

I joined together letters to make these words and phrases:

いつ	when
まいにち	every day
よく	often
ときどき	sometimes
きょう	today
あした	tomorrow

スポーツ	sport	を
サッカー	soccer	
クリケット	cricket	
フットボール	football	
テニス	tennis	
おんがく	music	particle O
どくしょ	reading	
コンピュータゲーム	computer games	
ショッピング	shopping	

しますか
Do (you) play/do?
します
(I) play/do
しません
(I) don't play/do

ぜんぜん	スポーツ	を	しません
not at all	sports	particle O	(I) don't play/do

Read the questions below, then add yes（はい）or no（いいえ）, a time word, and the correct verb ending to make the answer true for you.

一 まいにちスポーツをしますか。

[yes/no]、[time word] スポーツをしま [verb ending]。

二 ときどきすいえいをしますか。

[yes/no]、[time word] すいえいをしま [verb ending]。

三 よくショッピングをしますか。

[yes/no]、[time word] ショッピングをしま [verb ending]。

四 あしたテニスをしますか。

[yes/no]、[time word] テニスをしま [verb ending]。

五 きょうバスケットボールをしますか。

[yes/no]、[time word] バスケットボールをしま [verb ending]。

Are you ready to take the ultimate Japanese sentence challenge?
Make up a correct Japanese sentence and score it according to the following rules.

For each full stop, comma or small letter give yourself	1 point
For each hiragana letter give yourself	2 points
For each katakana letter (big or little) give yourself	3 points
For each particle は or particle を give yourself	4 points

Pipi has already done his. Have at look at his sentence and score, then try it yourself.

げ	つ	よ	う	び	に	テ	ニ	ス	を	し	ま	せ	ん	。	
2	2	2	2	2	2	3	3	3	4	2	2	2	2	1	**34**

Total= 34!!!

Use as many rows as you wish for each sentence. Add together your points and write your total point score at the end of each sentence.

sentence																	
points																	
sentence																	
points																	
sentence																	
points																	
sentence																	
points																	
sentence																	
points																	
sentence																	
points																	
sentence																	
points																	

Score goals

0–30	Good try!
31–50	I think you're getting the hang of it!
51–70	Are you sure you're not Japanese?
71+	You'd better apply for the job of Japanese teacher at your school!

どこ	where	で
がっこう	school	
こうえん	park	
うみ	beach/sea	
みせ	shop(s)	at
としょかん	library	
グランド	sports field	
うち	home	

スポーツ	sport	を
サッカー	soccer	
すいえい	swimming	
フットボール	football	
テニス	tennis	
べんきょう	study	particle o
どくしょ	reading	
コンピュータゲーム	computer games	
ショッピング	shopping	

しますか
Do (you) play/do?
します
(I) play/do
しません
(I) don't play/do

Complete the following sentences using the appropriate endings from the 'Sentence endings' box.

一 みせで ______

二 がっこうで ______

三 うみで ______

四 グランドで ______

五 としょかんで ______

Sentence endings:

フットボールをします。

ショッピングをします。

すいえいをします。

スポーツをしません。

べんきょうをします。

Now take each of the above sentences and include the person who is doing the activity and how often he/she does the activity. Then write what your sentence means in English underneath.

You may find these 'people' words useful:
せんせい – teacher　おかあさん – mother　おとうさん – father;
おにいさん – older brother　おねえさん – older sister

一 おねえさんは、よくみせでショッピングをします。

My older sister often does shopping at the shops.

二 ______

三 ______

四 ______

五 ______

Pipi has just received a letter from Mako (まこ), the daughter of the Kumamoto family Pipi will be staying with when he visits Japan. Read Mako's letter, which has been written in the traditional vertical style.

ピピちゃんへ

こんにちは。おげんきですか。わたしのなまえは、まこです。おおさかにすんでいます。六ねんせいです。十二さいです。にほんじんです。わたしのしゅみは、スポーツです。すいえいとテニスがだいすきです。どようびにすいえいをします。まいにちがっこうでテニスをします。じゅうどうは、あまりすきじゃないです。

まこより

Look at Mako's letter carefully, then finish Pipi's tips for writing downwards.

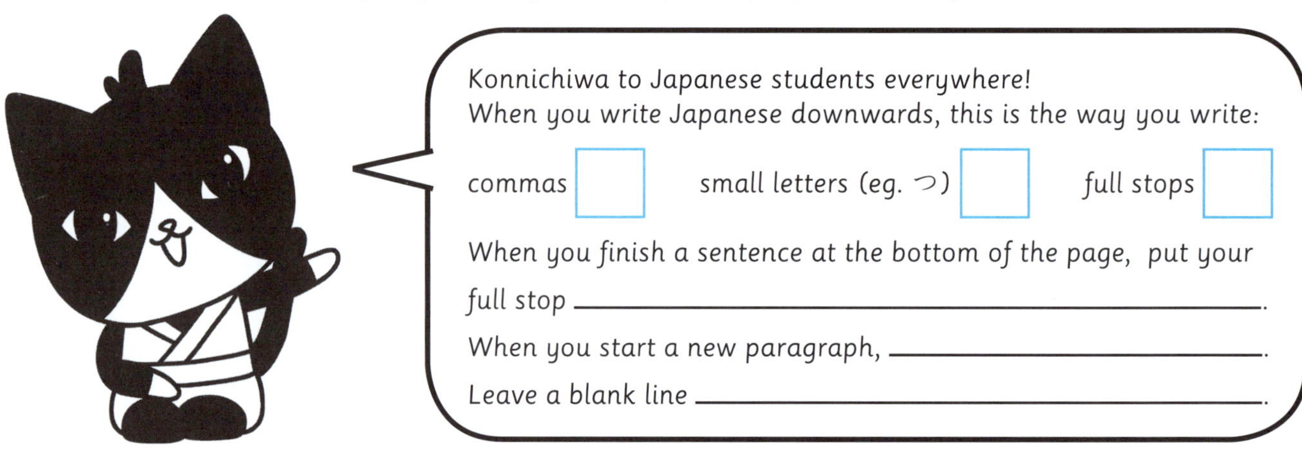

Now answer the following questions about Mako, writing your answers in the vertical style next to each question.

一 まこさんは、どこにすんでいますか。

二 まこさんは、なにじんですか。

三 まこさんは、テニスがすきですか。

四 まこさんは、いつすいえいをしますか。

百	ひゃく	100
二百	にひゃく	200
三百	さんびゃく	300
四百	よんひゃく	400
五百	ごひゃく	500
六百	ろっぴゃく	600
七百	ななひゃく	700
八百	はっぴゃく	800
九百	きゅうひゃく	900

十	じゅう	10
二十	にじゅう	20
三十	さんじゅう	30
四十	よんじゅう	40
五十	ごじゅう	50
六十	ろくじゅう	60
七十	（しち）ななじゅう	70
八十	はちじゅう	80
九十	きゅうじゅう	90

一	いち	1
二	に	2
三	さん	3
四	し / よん	4
五	ご	5
六	ろく	6
七	しち / なな	7
八	はち	8
九	く / きゅう	9

Look at the way we write Japanese numbers with hundreds in them. Trace over the grey numbers, then, when you are familiar with the pattern, fill in the blank boxes to complete the table.

324: 三百 plus 二十 plus 四 = 三百二十四

639: 六百 plus 三十 plus 九 = 六百三十九

161: 百 plus 六十 plus 一 = 百六十一

795: 七☐ plus 九十 plus 五 = 七☐九☐☐

288: 二百 plus 八☐ plus 八 = 二☐☐十☐

469: ☐☐ plus ☐☐ plus ☐ = ☐☐☐☐☐

514: ☐☐ plus ☐ plus ☐ = ☐☐☐☐

825: ☐☐ plus ☐☐ plus ☐ = ☐☐☐☐☐

344: ☐☐ plus ☐☐ plus ☐ = ☐☐☐☐☐

795: ☐☐ plus ☐☐ plus ☐ = ☐☐☐☐☐

If you find these numbers difficult, you will be pleased to know that Japanese people generally use our number system in normal daily life.

ONLY use the coordinates in dark blue boxes that have been written CORRECTLY to plot the hidden number in the grid below. Cross out the incorrect numbers.

728	七百二十八	エ	七
649	六百四十九	コ	三
299	二百九十八	ア	五
312	三百十二	ケ	十四
761	七百六十 一	ク	十四
435	四百三十五	キ	四
649	六百四十九	カ	十四
295	二百九十五	オ	十四
449	四百四十九	エ	三
568	五六百十八	キ	九
884	八百七十五	オ	七
935	九百三十五	ク	十七

724	七百二十四	コ	四
916	九百十十六	イ	九
583	五百八十三	コ	五
289	二百八十九	エ	五
397	三百九十七	ク	十一
267	二百六十七	キ	十四
345	三百四十五	サ	十四
632	六十三十二	セ	五
843	八百四十三	ク	十六
947	九百四十七	キ	六
286	二百七十六	ウ	五
376	三百七十六	コ	六

425	四百二十五	エ	六
338	三百三十八	ク	十五
945	九百九十五	シ	八
886	八百八十六	エ	四
259	二百五十九	ク	十三
237	二百三十七	コ	七
383	三百八十七	ス	八
698	六百九十八	キ	五
151	百五十一	エ	十四
458	四百五十八	ク	十二
789	七百八十九	コ	十四
925	九百三十五	ウ	十

Use the coordinates after the correctly written numbers (there is a katakana coordinate and a number coordinate), then shade the boxes where the two coordinates meet. When you have finished you will see a Japanese number.

セ																			
ス																			
シ																			
サ																			
コ																			
ケ																			
ク																			
キ																			
カ																			
オ																			
エ																			
ウ																			
イ																			
ア																			
	一	二	三	四	五	六	七	八	九	十	十一	十二	十三	十四	十五	十六	十七	十八	十九

The hidden number is

Japanese answer	English answer

千		
(一) 千	(いっ) せん	1000
二千	にせん	2000
三千	さんぜん	3000
四千	よんせん	4000
五千	ごせん	5000
六千	ろくせん	6000
七千	ななせん	7000
八千	はっせん	8000
九千	きゅうせん	9000

百	ひゃく	100
二百	にひゃく	200
三百	さんびゃく	300
四百	よんひゃく	400
五百	ごひゃく	500
六百	ろっぴゃく	600
七百	ななひゃく	700
八百	はっぴゃく	800
九百	きゅうひゃく	900

十	じゅう	10
二十	にじゅう	20
三十	さんじゅう	30
四十	よんじゅう	40
五十	ごじゅう	50
六十	ろくじゅう	60
七十	(しち) ななじゅう	70
八十	はちじゅう	80
九十	きゅうじゅう	90

一	いち	1
二	に	2
三	さん	3
四	し / よん	4
五	ご	5
六	ろく	6
七	しち / なな	7
八	はち	8
九	く / きゅう	9

The unit of currency in Japan is the yen. The symbol ¥ is used all over the world to mean Japanese yen. Ask your teacher roughly how many yen there are in $1.00.

$1.00 = ¥ ______

In Japan, yen is written in kanji like this 円 and is pronounced えん.
It is written after the number of yen, not before it.

¥250 = 二百五十円

Normally, prices are written using the ¥ symbol followed by the same kind of numbers we use, but sometimes prices are written the traditional way, especially in shops that sell traditional Japanese goods.

Look at the items in the table below and compare the prices. Write down which shop has the best price, and work out how much cheaper it is than the other shop.

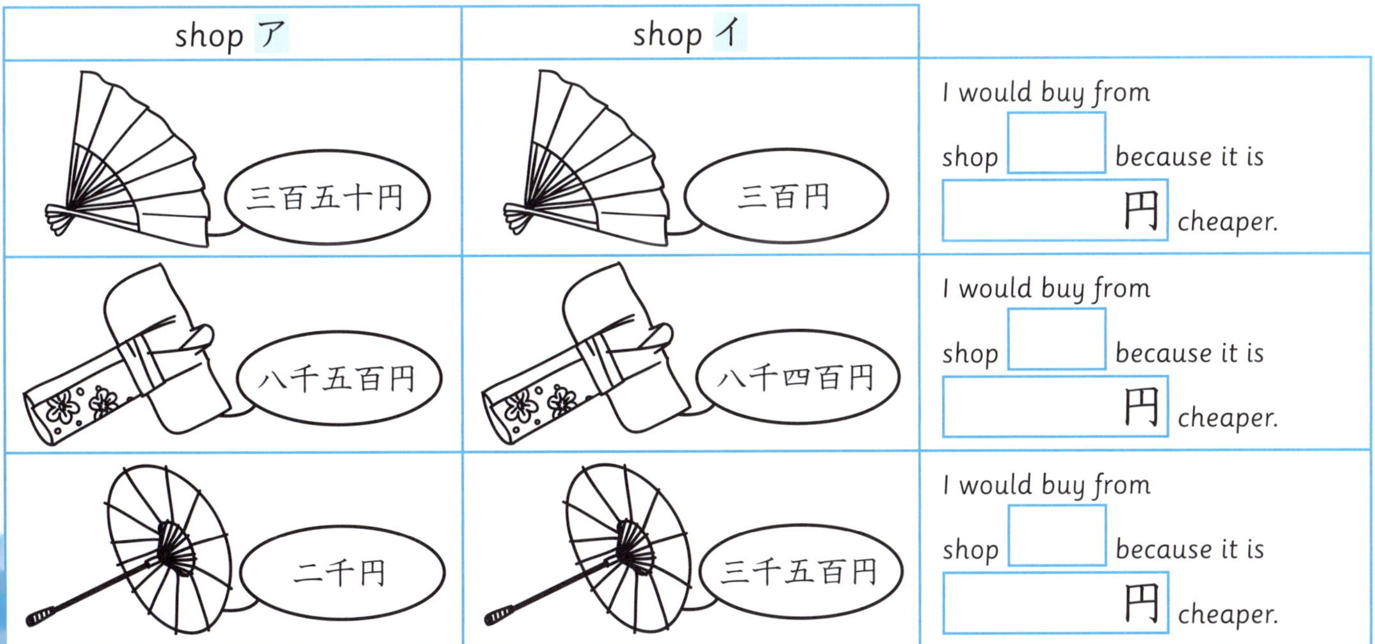

shop ア	shop イ	
三百五十円	三百円	I would buy from shop ☐ because it is ☐ 円 cheaper.
八千五百円	八千四百円	I would buy from shop ☐ because it is ☐ 円 cheaper.
二千円	三千五百円	I would buy from shop ☐ because it is ☐ 円 cheaper.

Answer the following questions using Japanese numbers.

一 What is the number before 八千九百九十九 ?

二 What is twice the number 三千八百 ?

三 Which number is 1/4 of 四千九百六十 ?

四 Which number is 5 more than 六千二百九 ?

五 How many minutes are there in 2 days?

六 Which number is 5000 more than 二千百五十八 ?

七 650 Japanese people took their shoes off and placed them in an empty shoe box. How many shoes were there in the box?

八 4432 bowls of noodles were served in a Japanese restaurant. How many chopsticks would have been provided?

九 3642 people boarded the Shinkansen (bullet train) in Tokyo. 523 people got off at the first station and no-one else got on the train. How many people were left?

十 523 Japanese people ate 2 yakitori chicken skewers each. The yakitori skewers had 4 pieces of grilled chicken each. How many pieces of grilled chicken were consumed?

Write the following numbers in Japanese.

7389		8569	
9276		2493	
4456		1876	
2988		4070	
5218		2934	

これ	は
this	
それ	
that	
あれ	particle WA
that (over there)	

いらっしゃいませ。
Welcome (to my shop).
すみません が、…
Excuse me, but …

いくら です か。
How much is it?
☺☺☺ 円 です。
It's ☺☺☺ yen.

そう です か。	Is that so?
☺☺☺ を ください。	May I have ☺☺☺ please?
ありがとう ございます。	Thank you very much.

Tim (ティム) has been mowing his neighbours' lawns to make some extra money. He now has enough to buy a present for his older sister. Fill in the blank boxes below to complete the shopping conversation between Tim and the salesperson.

Here is a picture of the famous golden pavilion (きんかくじ) in Kyoto. Use the grid coordinates to help you copy it onto the grid below, then colour in your picture.

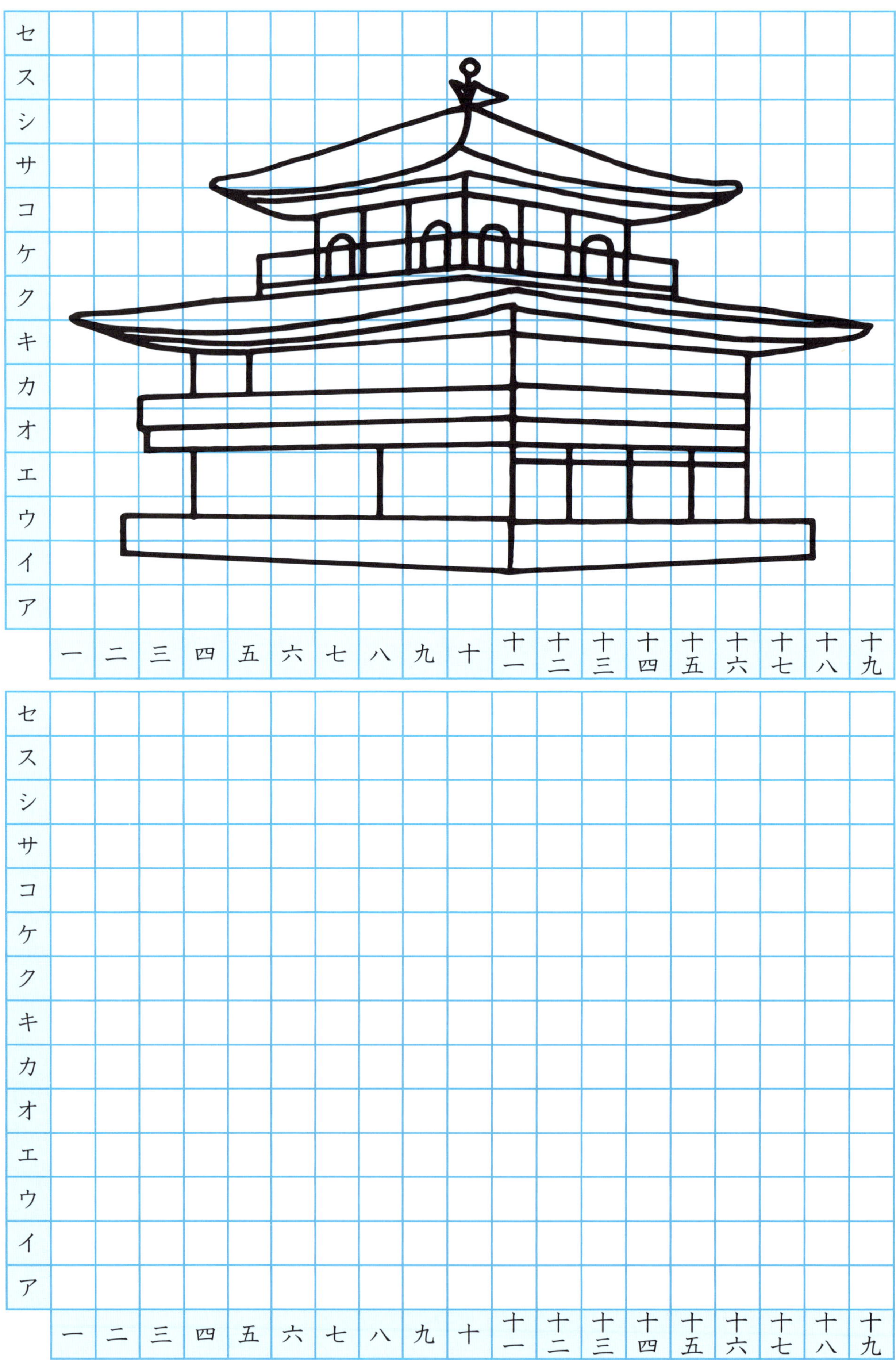

これ / this	は / particle WA
それ / that	
あれ / that (over there)	

いい	good
おもしろい	interesting/funny
かわいい	cute
たのしい	fun/enjoyable
つまらない	boring
おおきい	big
ちいさい	small

です	ね
is	isn't it?

そう です ね。	Yes it is, isn't it?

Pipi (ピピちゃん) and Fifi (フィフィちゃん) are looking at Pipi's photos from his trip to Japan. (It looks like Pipi had a visitor during his trip!) Write their comments underneath each photo in the space provided. The first photo has been done for you to trace over.

ピ： いいですね。
フィ： そうですね。

ピ：
フィ：

ピ：
フィ：

ピ：
フィ：

Use the boxes below to make your own shopping cartoon/manga. Choose your characters (you may choose people, animals or non-living things), then decide what kind of shop you are in and what your characters will say. Put the speech in speech bubbles. Use as many boxes as you need.

いつ	when
まいにち	everyday
よく	often
ときどき	sometimes
きょう	today
あした	tomorrow
ぜんぜん	not at all

なに	what	を
ほん	book	
まんが	cartoon, comic	
テレビゲーム	video game	
コンピュータゲーム	computer game	particle O
うた	song	

かいます か
Do (you) buy? / Will (you) buy?
かいます
(I) buy / (I) will buy
かいません
(I) don't buy

Heath

まんがは、あまりすきじゃないです。

まいにちほんをかいます。

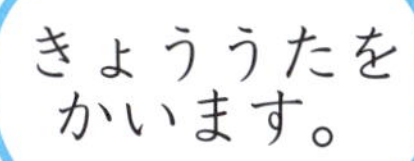

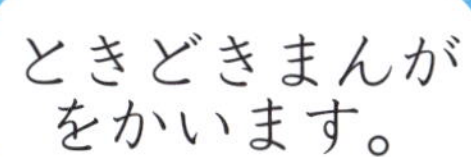

Using the students' statements above as clues, guess which student gave each of the answers below when they were questioned by their teacher. Draw the face of the student next to the answer you think they would have given.

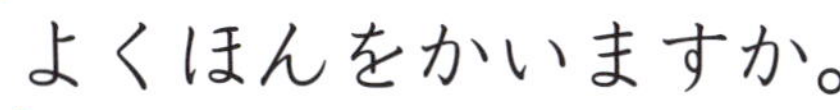

はい、よくほんをかいます。

うたをかいます。

コンピュータゲームをかいますか。

いいえ、コンピュータゲームをかいません。

うたをかいますか。

いいえ、うたをかいません。
まんがをかいます。

まんがをかいますか。

いいえ、ぜんぜんまんがをかいません。

Can you work out what these katakana words might be? They all come from English. Write what you think they mean in the blank boxes, then use each word in a sentence of your choice.

一 メニュー

二 クリスマス

三 コーンフレーク

四 カンガルー

五 ソフトボール

六 ペット

七 ホッケー

八 ダンス

九 チーズ

十 バンジージャンプ

ほん	book
まんが	cartoon, comic
テレビゲーム	video game
コンピュータゲーム	computer game
うた	song
にほんご	Japanese

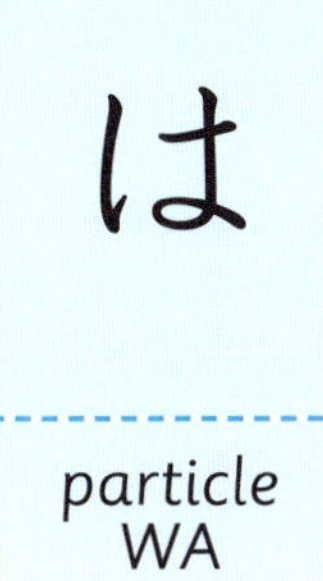

いいです	よかったです
is good	was good
おもしろいです	おもしろかったです
is interesting/funny	was interesting/funny
かわいいです	かわいかったです
is cute	was cute
たのしいです	たのしかったです
is fun/enjoyable	was fun/enjoyable
つまらないです	つまらなかったです
is boring	was boring

☺☺☺ は、どうです か。	How is it? (What's it like?)
☺☺☺ は、どうでした か。	How was it? (What was it like?)

Read the little stories below, then write an appropriate sentence in each speech bubble.

一 Pipi is reading a book. The せんせい asks him:
ほんは、どうですか。
What would Pipi reply?

二 Akiko went shopping yesterday.
She bought a new computer game. Her mother asks her:
コンピュータゲーム は、どうでしたか。
What would Akiko reply?

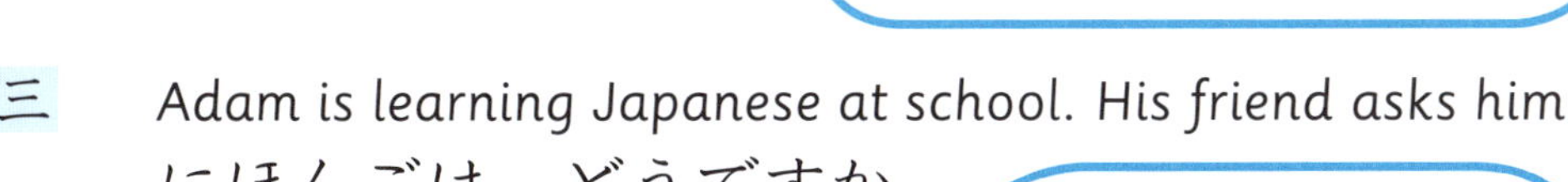

三 Adam is learning Japanese at school. His friend asks him:
にほんごは、どうですか。
What would Adam reply?

四 Yoshi listened to a new song yesterday by his favourite band. Today his friend asked him:
うたは、どうでしたか。
What would Yoshi reply?

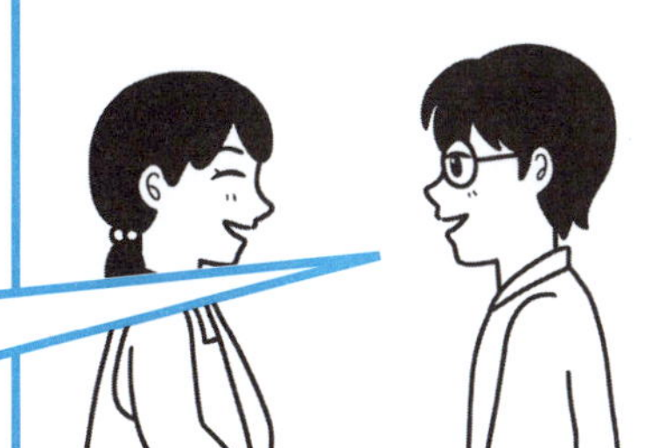

What is your opinion of different kinds of activities? Write a short composition on each of the topics below, then share your opinion with the class. The first one has been done by Pipi, as a guide.

スポーツ

ぼくは、スポーツがだいすきです。よく
スポーツをします。まいにちがっこうでス
ポーツをします。きょうテニスとすいえい
をします。あしたフットボールをします。
スポーツは、おもしろいです。

コンピュータゲーム

どくしょ

どこ	where	で
デパート	department store	
がっこう	school	at

きのう	yesterday
そして	and then
そうです か。	Is that so? / Really?
たのしかった です。	It was fun.

なに	を
what	
ほん	
book	
アイスクリーム	
ice-cream	
ジュース	particle o
juice	
スポーツ	
sport	
にほんご	
Japanese (language)	

か	?

かいます	かいました
(I) buy / (I) will buy	(I) bought
よみます	よみました
(I) read / (I) will read	(I) read
たべます	たべました
(I) eat / (I) will eat	(I) ate
のみます	のみました
(I) drink / (I) will drink	I drank
します	しました
(I) do / (I) will do	(I) did
べんきょう します	べんきょう しました
(I) study / (I) will study	(I) studied

On Saturday morning, Pipi and his mother discussed what Pipi did the day before. Use the information in the dialogue to complete the blanks in Pipi's diary for Friday.

ほんをかいました。

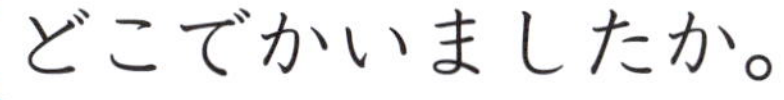

デパートでかいました。

そうですか。デパートで
なにをたべましたか。

そしてジュースをのみました。

もくようび

がっこうでにほんごを
べんきょうしました。
そしてスポーツを
しました。たのしかった
です。

きんようび

[ ] で
ほんを [ ] ました。
[ ] を
たべました。そして
ジュース [ ] のみました。

Create your own dialogue and diary entry, just like the ones on the previous page. Draw in your own characters and use as many different sentence patterns as you can.

In the box below, show how Japanese verbs change when we are talking about something that happens now or will happen in the future, compared with talking about something that happened in the past.

CHANGING VERBS FROM THE PRESENT TENSE TO THE PAST TENSE

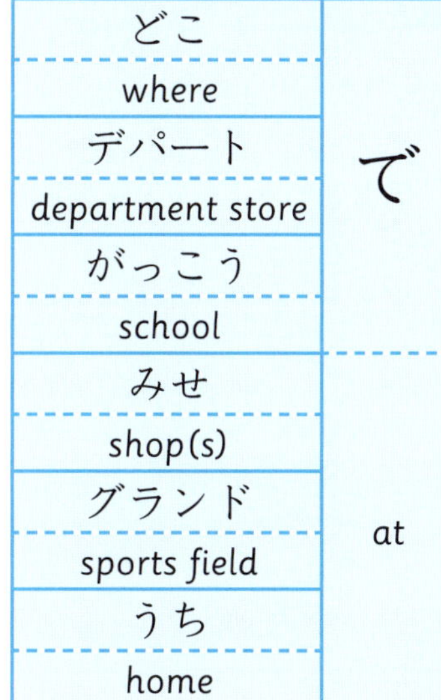

where		
どこ where	で at	
デパート department store		
がっこう school		
みせ shop(s)		
グランド sports field		
うち home		

who		
だれ who	と with	
ともだち friend		
☺☺☺ さん girl's name		
☺☺☺ くん boy's name		
おかあさん mother		
おとうさん father		

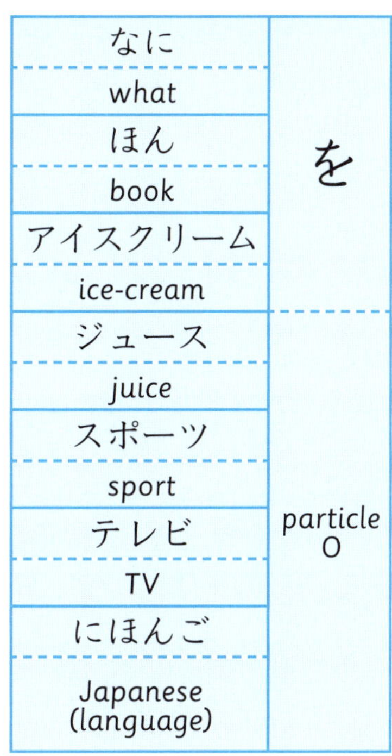

what		
なに what	を particle O	
ほん book		
アイスクリーム ice-cream		
ジュース juice		
スポーツ sport		
テレビ TV		
にほんご Japanese (language)		

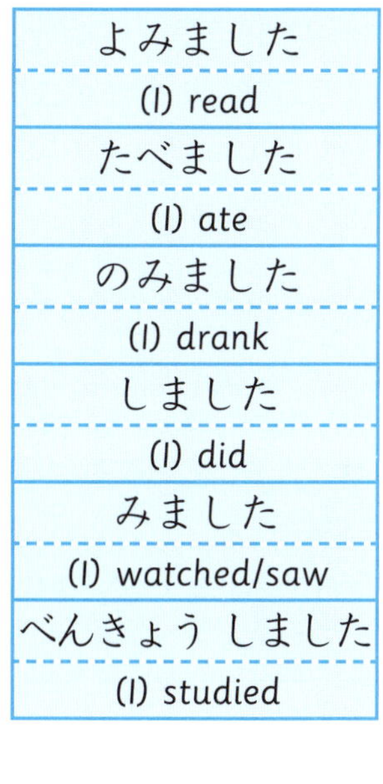

verb
よみました (I) read
たべました (I) ate
のみました (I) drank
しました (I) did
みました (I) watched/saw
べんきょう しました (I) studied

Choose words to insert in the blank boxes below to make your own personalised story. Practise reading it, then present it to the class if you have time. Illustrate your story in the boxes underneath.

こんにちは。＿＿＿＿ のなまえは、＿＿＿＿
です。＿＿＿＿ にすんでいます。
＿＿＿＿ じんです。＿＿＿＿ さいです。
＿＿＿＿ ねんせいです。＿＿＿＿ ようびに
＿＿＿＿ で ＿＿＿＿ をかいました。
＿＿＿＿ ようびに ＿＿＿＿ と ＿＿＿＿ を
かいました。＿＿＿＿ ようびに ＿＿＿＿ で
＿＿＿＿ とアイスクリームを ＿＿＿＿ 。
そして ＿＿＿＿ ようびに ＿＿＿＿ を
＿＿＿＿ 。

＿＿＿＿ ようび	＿＿＿＿ ようび	＿＿＿＿ ようび	＿＿＿＿ ようび

Transform sentence 一 into sentence 四 by changing one word **only** each time you rewrite the sentence. The first one has been done for you to trace over.

ア

一 がっこうでともだちとほんをよみました。

二 がっこうではなさんとほんをよみました。

三 がっこうではなさんとほんをかいました。

四 デパートではなさんとほんをかいました。

Translate the last sentence into English:

____

イ

一 グランドでたかくんとフットボールをしました。

二

三

四 がっこうでともだちとフットボールをみました。

Translate the last sentence into English:

____

ウ

一 きんようびにがっこうでともだちとテレビをみました。

二

三

四 げつようびにうちでおとうさんとテレビをみました。

Translate the last sentence into English:

____

Can you remember these words? Write them in Japanese.

yellow		sometimes	
mother		this	
Saturday		(I) study	
(I) read		Japanese language	

どこ / where	に / to
デパート / department store	
がっこう / school	
みせ / shop(s)	
グランド / sports field	
うみ / sea/beach	

いきます / will go / go	か
いきました / went	?

どうです か。	How is it?
どうでした か。	How was it?
なに を しました か。	What did (you) do?

たのしい です	is fun
たのしかった です	was fun
おもしろい です	is interesting/funny
おもしろかった です	was interesting/funny
つまらない です	is boring
つまらなかった です	was boring

Look at Tim's diary from part of last week, then help him answer the teacher's questions.

すいようび	もくようび	きんようび	どようび	にちようび
がっこうに いきました。がっこうでほんをよみました。おもしろいです。	みせに いきました。みせで えんぴつを かいました。	がっこうに いきました。がっこうで にほんごを べんきょうしました。おもしろかったです。	グランドに いきました。グランドで サッカーを しました。たのしかったです。	うみに いきました。うみですいえいをしました。たのしかったです。

ティムくん、もくようびにどこにいきましたか。

もくようびに ☐☐ に ☐☐☐☐☐。

みせでなにをしましたか。

みせで ☐☐☐☐ を ☐☐☐☐☐。

にちようびにどこにいきましたか。

☐☐☐☐☐ に う み に ☐☐☐☐☐。

どうでしたか。

☐☐☐☐☐☐☐☐。

Translate the following words/phrases into Japanese, then copy the corresponding puzzle fragment into the the grid at the bottom of the page to find the hidden hiragana letter. You must copy each puzzle fragment into the square with the same letter as the shaded letter in your answer.

library

Wednesday

fun

mother

was good

(I) go

friend

music

の	た	お
も		よ
ん	さ	ま

What is the hidden hiragana letter?

Place		Particle
こうえん	park	に (to)
がっこう	school	に (to)
デパート	department store	に (to)
としょかん	library	に (to)
グランド	sports field	に (to)
うみ	sea/beach	に (to)

Person		Particle
ともだち	friend	と (with)
☺☺☺ さん	girl's name	と (with)
☺☺☺ くん	boy's name	と (with)
おかあさん	mother	と (with)
おとうさん	father	と (with)

いきます	will go / go
いきました	went
いきません	will not go / do not go
いきませんでした	did not go

Read the information about the characters below, then write ほんとう (true) next to the true statements and うそ (a lie) next to the false statements.

Pipi (ピピちゃん)	Akiko (あきこさん)	Adam (アダム)	Fifi (フィフィちゃん)
としょかんにいきました。ともだちといきました。	がっこうにいきませんでした。デパートにいきました。	グランドにいきませんでした。ともだちとこうえんにいきました。	うみにいきました。せんせいといきました。

一 あきこさんは、デパートにいきませんでした。 ______

二 フィフィちゃんは、うみにせんせいといきました。 ______

三 ピピちゃんは、としょかんにともだちといきませんでした。 ______

四 アダムは、こうえんにいきました。 ______

五 フィフィちゃんは、うみにいきませんでした。 ______

Complete the crossword puzzle by translating the clues below or supplying the missing words. Don't use punctuation (full stops etc.)!

1.						2.		3.		4.		
			5.		6.		7.					
		8.										9.
10.			11.									
12.												
									13.		14.	
15.						16.						
			17.								18.	
					19.							
									20.	21.		
22.								23.				
			24.									
25.							26.					

Clues across

1. hobby
2. ほん □ よみます。
4. good
5. おげんき [ ]。 (How are you?)
7. music
10. I didn't go to school.
14. what
15. who
16. hello (good day)
17. yen
18. book
19. テニスを [ ]。 (Do you play tennis?)
20. park
22. [ ] ようび (Friday)
23. Isn't it?
24. everyday
25. にほんごが [ ]。 (I like Japanese.)
26. Will you buy?

Clues down

1. 7 (in hiragana)
3. 3 (in hiragana)
4. How much is it?
6. It's cute!
7. What's your name?
8. where
9. I'm Japanese (girl)
11. (I) swim at the beach.
12. (I) go with my friend.
13. 8 (in hiragana)
19. [ ] してください。 (Please be quiet.)
21. It's the beach.

A	フ	ア	ア	ア	ア	ア	ア						ア
✍													
I	ノ	イ	イ	イ	イ	イ	イ						イ
✍													
U	'	' '	ウ	ウ	ウ	ウ	ウ						ウ
✍													
E	一	丅	エ	エ	エ	エ	エ						エ
✍													
O	一	十	オ	オ	オ	オ	オ						オ
✍													

Trace over the grey katakana letters, then fill in the blank boxes. Use the wordlist at the back of the book if you need to.

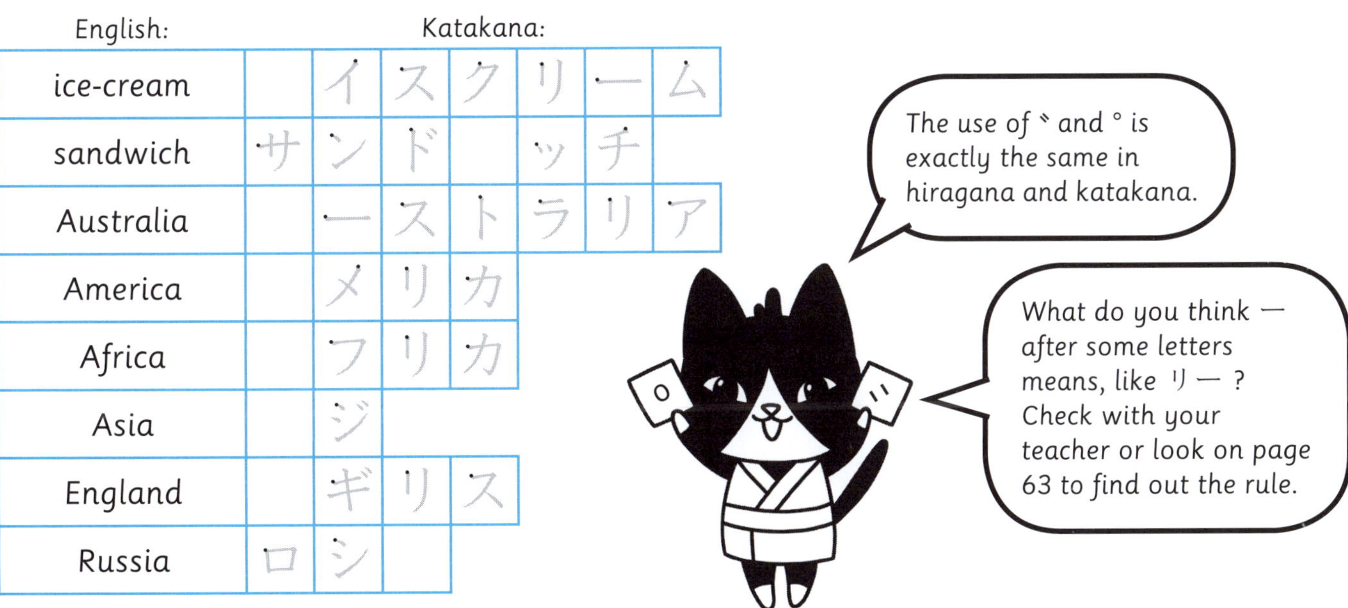

English:	Katakana:						
ice-cream		イ	ス	ク	リ	ー	ム
sandwich	サ	ン	ド		ッ	チ	
Australia		ー	ス	ト	ラ	リ	ア
America		メ	リ	カ			
Africa		フ	リ	カ			
Asia		ジ					
England		ギ	リ	ス			
Russia	ロ	シ					

The use of ゛ and ° is exactly the same in hiragana and katakana.

What do you think ー after some letters means, like リー ? Check with your teacher or look on page 63 to find out the rule.

Write the matching hiragana letter for each katakana letter.

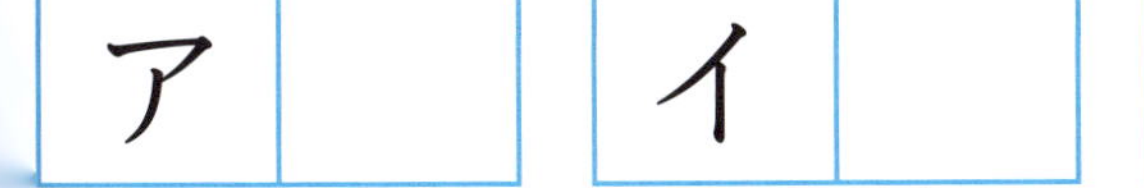

ア		イ		ウ		エ		オ	

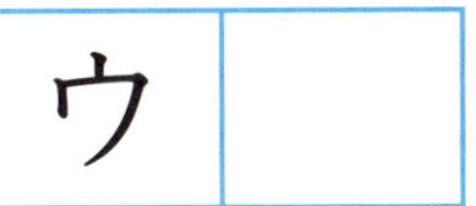

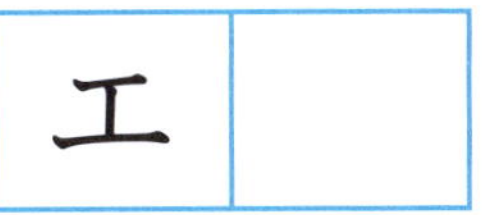

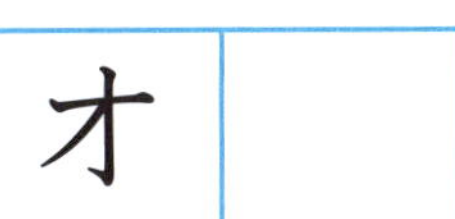

Put the following sets of words into the correct order to make complete sentences. Translate each sentence into English.

一	Japanese jumbled words	を　たべます　サンドイッチ
	Japanese sentence	
	English sentence	

二	Japanese jumbled words	いきます　アメリカ　に
	Japanese sentence	
	English sentence	

三	Japanese jumbled words	すんでいます　に　ロシア
	Japanese sentence	
	English sentence	

四	Japanese jumbled words	アイスクリーム　です　がすき
	Japanese sentence	
	English sentence	

Now use these words to make sentences of your own.

一	Japanese jumbled words	オーストラリア
	Japanese sentence	
	English sentence	

二	Japanese jumbled words	イギリス
	Japanese sentence	
	English sentence	

三	Japanese jumbled words	アフリカ
	Japanese sentence	
	English sentence	

KA	フ	カ	カ	カ	カ	カ	カ						カ
GA	ガ	ガ	ガ	ガ	ガ	ガ	ガ						ガ
KI	一	二	キ	キ	キ	キ	キ						キ
GI	ギ	ギ	ギ	ギ	ギ	ギ	ギ						ギ
KU	ノ	ク	ク	ク	ク	ク	ク						ク
GU	グ	グ	グ	グ	グ	グ	グ						グ
KE	ノ	𠂉	ケ	ケ	ケ	ケ	ケ						ケ
GE	ゲ	ゲ	ゲ	ゲ	ゲ	ゲ	ゲ						ゲ
KO	フ	コ	コ	コ	コ	コ	コ						コ
GO	ゴ	ゴ	ゴ	ゴ	ゴ	ゴ	ゴ						ゴ

The items below are written using katakana letters. Did you know that katakana is used for words that come from English? Can you work out which katakana letters are missing? Write them in the blank boxes and trace over the other katakana letters.

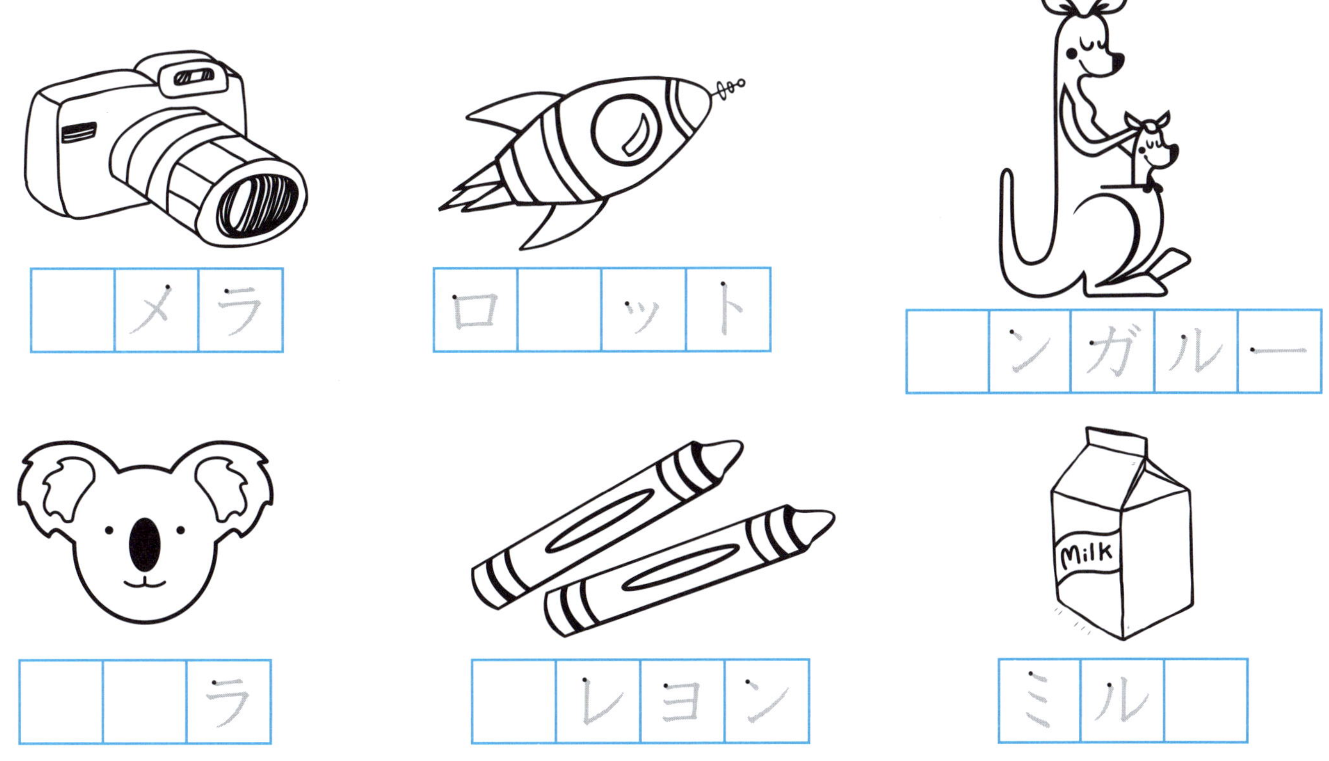

Below are some more Japanese loan words that come from English. Each of the words is also written in hiragana and English. Join the matching katakana, hiragana and English words with a line and shade them in the same colour.

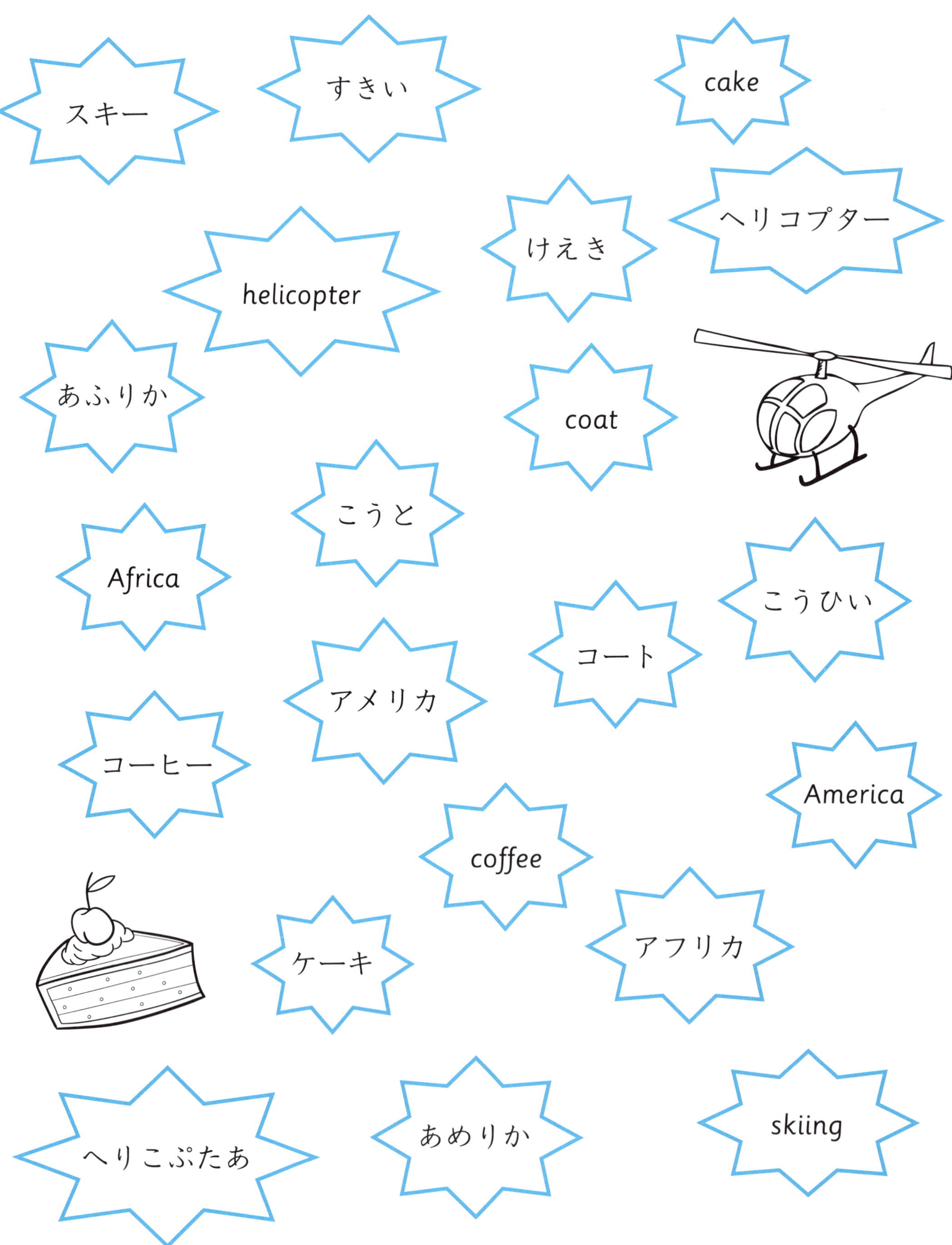

SA	一	十	サ	サ	サ	サ	サ						サ
ZA	ザ	ザ	ザ	ザ	ザ	ザ	ザ						ザ
SHI	`	゛	シ	シ	シ	シ	シ						シ
JI	ジ	ジ	ジ	ジ	ジ	ジ	ジ						ジ
SU	フ	ス	ス	ス	ス	ス	ス						ス
ZU	ズ	ズ	ズ	ズ	ズ	ズ	ズ						ズ
SE	一	セ	セ	セ	セ	セ	セ						セ
ZE	ゼ	ゼ	ゼ	ゼ	ゼ	ゼ	ゼ						ゼ
SO	`	ソ	ソ	ソ	ソ	ソ	ソ						ソ
ZO	ゾ	ゾ	ゾ	ゾ	ゾ	ゾ	ゾ						ゾ

Using each of the loan words at the bottom of the page once only, fill in the blank spaces in each sentence so that it makes sense.

一 ＿＿＿＿＿ にいきます。

二 ＿＿＿＿＿ がすきです。

三 しゅみは ＿＿＿＿＿ です。

四 ＿＿＿＿＿ をたべます。

五 ＿＿＿＿＿ じんです。

Katakana loan words:

サッカー　ケーキ　サーカス
アジア　スイス

Use your ruler to draw straight lines between the matching hiragana and katakana letters written outside the frame. Then colour ONLY the sections with サ in them to reveal the hidden katakana letter.

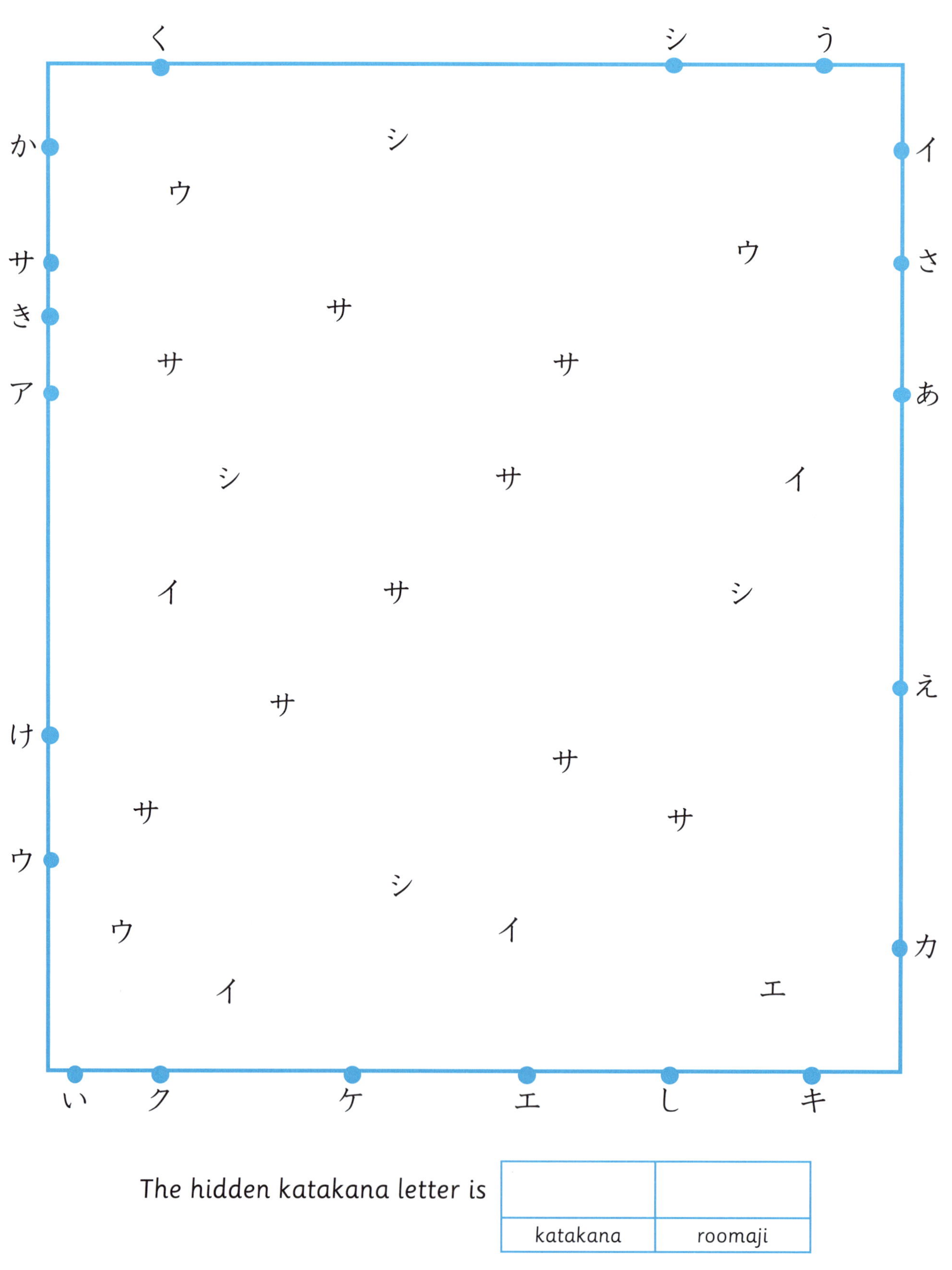

The hidden katakana letter is

katakana	roomaji

TA	ノ	ク	タ	タ	タ	タ	タ					タ
DA	ダ	ダ	ダ	ダ	ダ	ダ	ダ					ダ
CHI	ノ	二	チ	チ	チ	チ	チ					チ
TSU	丶	丶丶	ツ	ツ	ツ	ツ	ツ					ツ
TE	一	二	テ	テ	テ	テ	テ					テ
DE	デ	デ	デ	デ	デ	デ	デ					デ
TO	丨	ト	ト	ト	ト	ト	ト					ト
DO	ド	ド	ド	ド	ド	ド	ド					ド

Each of the following katakana letters is missing a stroke. Add the stroke, then write the matching hiragana letter in the blank box next to the katakana letter.

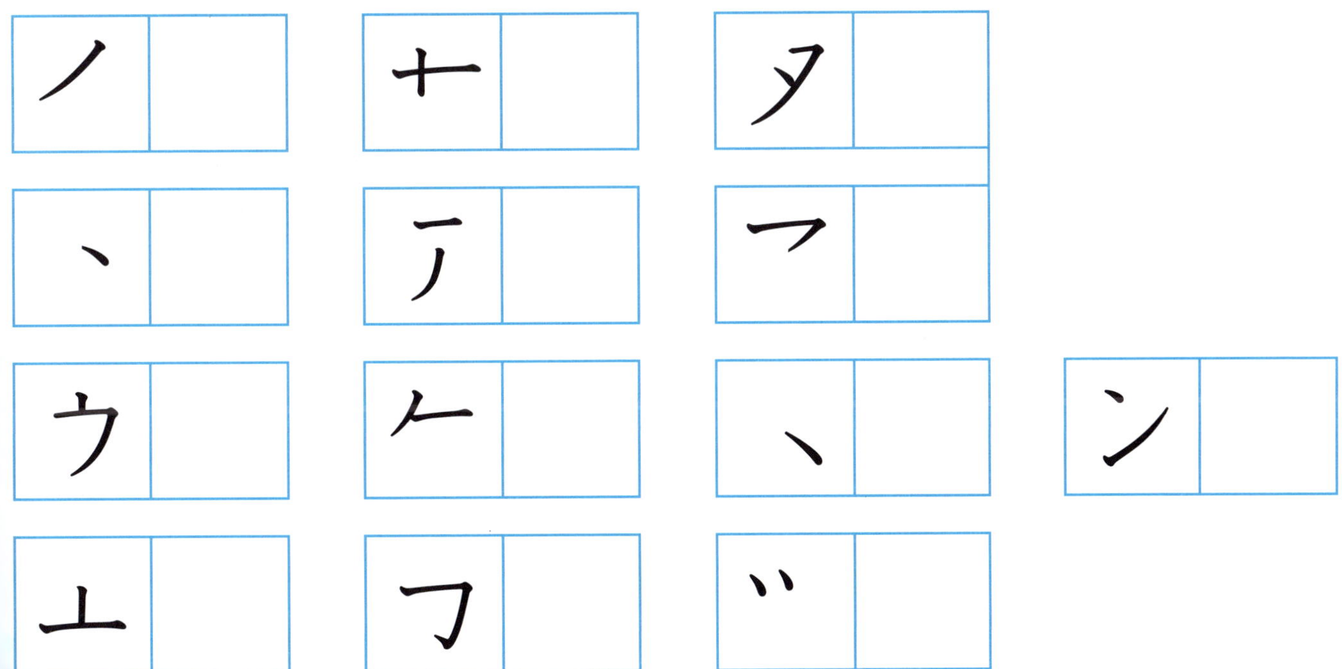

Follow the alphabet from ア to ト to complete the dot-to-dot puzzle.

NA	ー	ナ	ナ	ナ	ナ	ナ	ナ						ナ
NI	ー	ニ	ニ	ニ	ニ	ニ	ニ						ニ
NU	フ	ヌ	ヌ	ヌ	ヌ	ヌ	ヌ						ヌ
NE	ˋ	ラ	ネ	ネ	ネ	ネ	ネ						ネ
NO	ノ	ノ	ノ	ノ	ノ	ノ	ノ						ノ

Read the katakana loan word, then fill in the missing letters in the matching English word underneath.

ノート
noteb _ _ k

トースト
toa _ _

テニスコート
_ _ _ _ _ is _ our _

ネクタイ
neckt _ _

ナッツ
_ _ ts

ココア
c _ c _ a

ナース
_ ur _ e

インドネシア
In _ _ _ es _ _

ケーキ
c _ _ e

チータ
_ _ _ _ tah

タクシー
t _ x _

テスト
t _ _ t

カナダ
C _ n _ _ _

KATAKANA QUICK QUIZ – CIRCLE THE CORRECT ANSWER.

See how many of these questions you can answer. Check your answers with your friends.

一 How do you write 'JI' in katakana?

ギ　シ　ジ

二 How do you write 'KA A' in katakana?

カア　カー　カウ

三 What does カヌー mean in English?

custard　cunning　canoe

四 Which of the following things would you write on?

カード　イースター　チータ

五 Which of the following things can you eat?

コート　クッキー　コスト

六 What are you doing right now?

クイズ　セット　テスト

七 How do you write 'shiitsu' ('sheets') in katakana?

ツーシ　シイツ　シーツ

八 What do you eat at your birthday party?

ステーキ　ケーキ　ゲート

九 Which of the following things can't you hear?

ノック　ネット　ノイズ

十 Which of the following things would you wear in the sea?

コート　トースター　ウエットスーツ

WRITING LESSON 6 KATAKANA: HA HI FU HE HO

HA	ノ	ハ	ハ	ハ	ハ	ハ	ハ					ハ
BA	バ	バ	バ	バ	バ	バ	バ					バ
PA	パ	パ	パ	パ	パ	パ	パ					パ
HI	ー	ヒ	ヒ	ヒ	ヒ	ヒ	ヒ					ヒ
BI	ビ	ビ	ビ	ビ	ビ	ビ	ビ					ビ
PI	ピ	ピ	ピ	ピ	ピ	ピ	ピ					ピ
FU	フ	フ	フ	フ	フ	フ	フ					フ
BU	ブ	ブ	ブ	ブ	ブ	ブ	ブ					ブ
PU	プ	プ	プ	プ	プ	プ	プ					プ
HE	ヘ	ヘ	ヘ	ヘ	ヘ	ヘ	ヘ					ヘ
BE	ベ	ベ	ベ	ベ	ベ	ベ	ベ					ベ
PE	ペ	ペ	ペ	ペ	ペ	ペ	ペ					ペ
HO	一	十	才	ホ	ホ	ホ	ホ					ホ
BO	ボ	ボ	ボ	ボ	ボ	ボ	ボ					ボ
PO	ポ	ポ	ポ	ポ	ポ	ポ	ポ					ポ

Join the matching katakana loan words and English words with a line.

ヒーター	hard
ハード	hippie
ヘッドホン	high tech
ハイテク	heater
ヒッピー	hedge
ヘッジ	headphone

In the sentences below, the Japanese loan words have been written using hiragana letters by mistake. Colour in the loan words, then rewrite the sentences, changing the loan words from hiragana to katakana. Write what your sentence means in English.

一
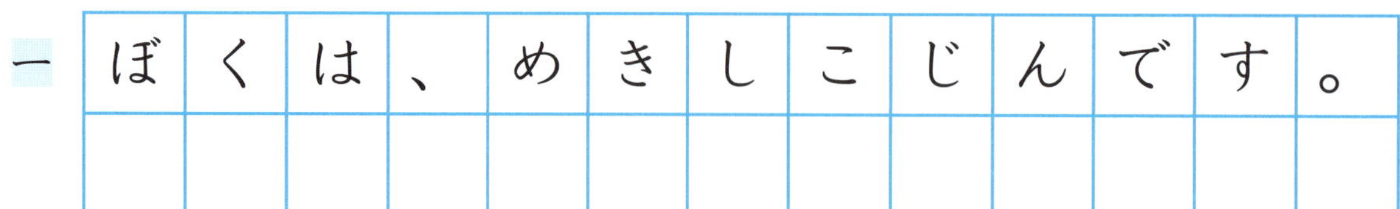

English: ______________________________

二
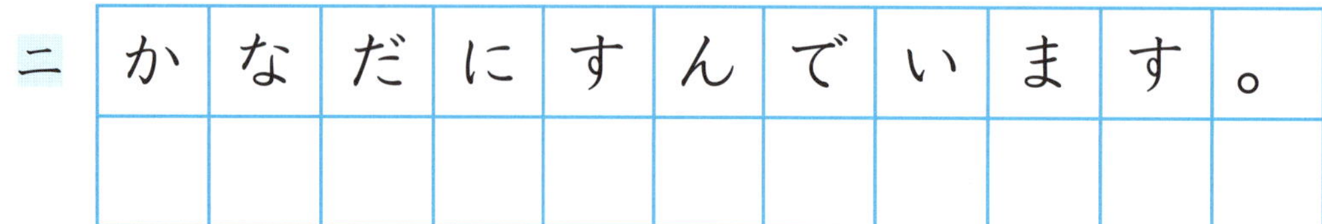

English: ______________________________

三
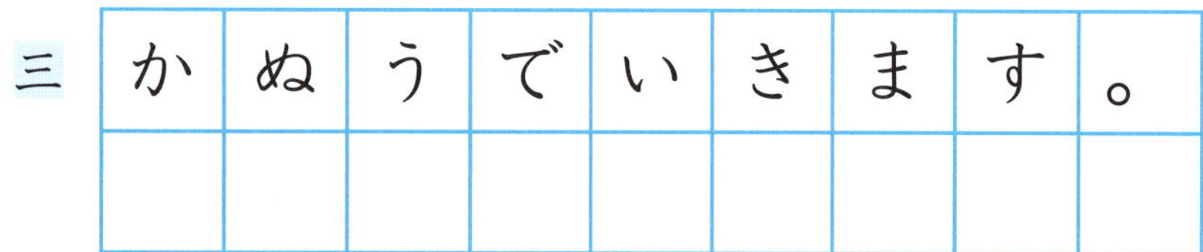

English: ______________________________

四
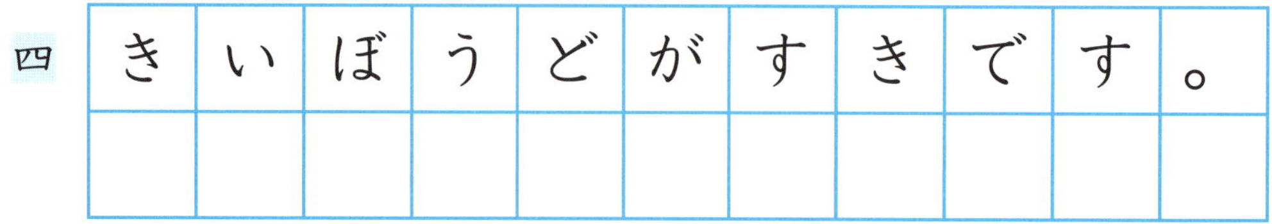

English: ______________________________

五 えっぐをたべます。

English: ______________________________

六
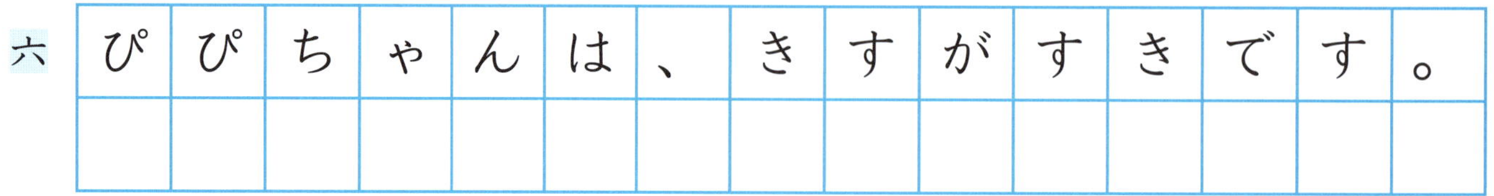

English: ______________________________

MA	マ	マ	マ	マ	マ	マ	マ						マ
✍													
MI	ミ	ミ	ミ	ミ	ミ	ミ	ミ						ミ
✍													
MU	ム	ム	ム	ム	ム	ム	ム						ム
✍													
ME	メ	メ	メ	メ	メ	メ	メ						メ
✍													
MO	モ	モ	モ	モ	モ	モ	モ						モ
✍													

You have encountered many katakana words by now and you should be getting to know the way that English words are changed into Japanese loan words. Try changing the following English words into katakana loan words, then compare your words with the correct answers at the bottom of page 58.

一 mood

二 mousse

三 monkey

四 motor

五 motto

六 Mister

七 mistake

八 miniskirt

九 mixer

十 maker

Follow the tangled lines from one katakana letter to the next to find the four mystery loan words, then join them to their correct English match with a line.

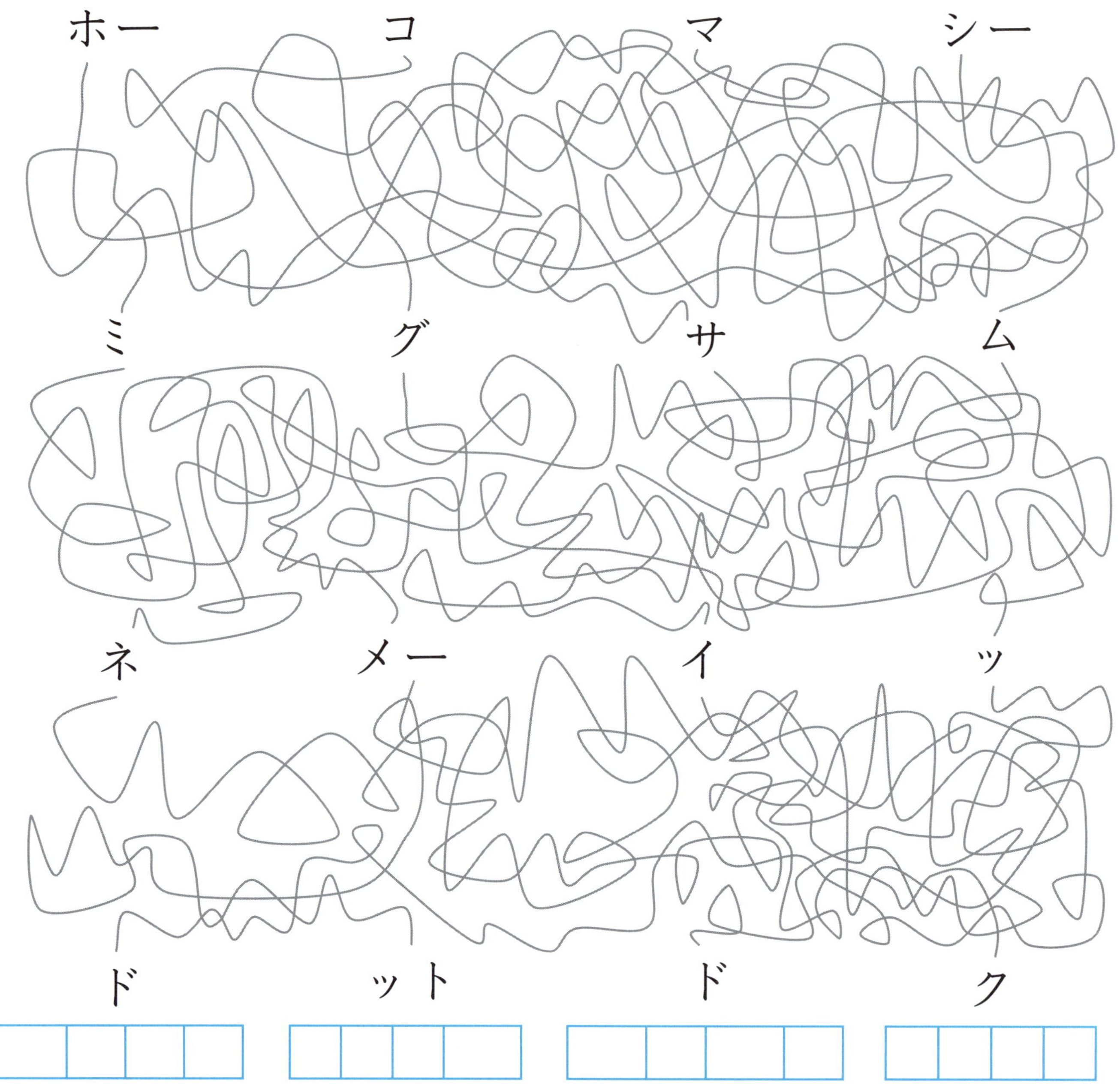

magnet comic seaside homemade

Answers to questions on p. 57

一	ムード	六	ミスター
二	ムース	七	ミステーク
三	モンキー	八	ミニスカート
四	モーター	九	ミキサー
五	モットー	十	メーカー

YA	ー	ヤ	ヤ	ヤ	ヤ	ヤ	ヤ						ヤ
YU	フ	ユ	ユ	ユ	ユ	ユ	ユ						ユ
YO	フ	ヨ	ヨ	ヨ	ヨ	ヨ	ヨ						ヨ

Complete the combination-sound katakana grid below. Remember that the rules are exactly the same as for hiragana letters. You use the 'i' form of each katakana group and add a small 'ya' (ヤ), 'yu' (ユ) or 'yo' (ヨ).

	small YA (ヤ)		small YU (ユ)		small YO (ヨ)	
K (キ)	キャ	KYA	キュ	KYU	キョ	KYO
G (ギ)		GYA		GYU		GYO
S (シ)		SHA		SHU		SHO
J (ジ)		JA		JU		JO
CH (チ)		CHA		CHU		CHO
N (ニ)		NYA		NYU		NYO
H (ヒ)		HYA		HYU		HYO
B (ビ)		BYA		BYU		BYO
P (ピ)		PYA		PYU		PYO
M (ミ)		MYA		MYU		MYO
R (リ)		RYA		RYU		RYO

Circle the odd one out! Use the hiragana letter clues under each odd one out to discover the name of Japan's national flower. Use the letters in the order in which they appear.

一	カヌー	ヨット	カナダ	カー
clues:	（き）	（め）	（さ）	（れ）
二	キュート	サイダー	コーヒー	ジュース
clues:	（く）	（り）	（ん）	（だ）
三	シャツ	クイズ	ネクタイ	ジャケット
clues:	（い）	（ら）	（ふ）	（ぬ）
四	ドーナツ	ケーキ	パイ	ゲーム
clues:	（え）	（そ）	（び）	（の）
五	サッカー	キス	テニス	スポーツ
clues:	（か）	（は）	（と）	（を）
六	キヨスク	ヨットハーバー	テニスコート	タイヤ
clues:	（ゆ）	（け）	（し）	（な）

RA	一	ラ	ラ	ラ	ラ	ラ	ラ						ラ
RI	丨	リ	リ	リ	リ	リ	リ						リ
RU	ノ	ル	ル	ル	ル	ル	ル						ル
RE	レ	レ	レ	レ	レ	レ	レ						レ
RO	丨	𠃍	ロ	ロ	ロ	ロ	ロ						ロ

How well do you know your katakana letters? Challenge yourself with the following questions.

一 Which katakana letters are the same as their hiragana matches?

二 Which katakana letters are the same as their hiragana matches after you remove one stroke?

三 Which katakana letter looks like a square? Write your answer in roomaji.

四 Which katakana letters have four strokes?

五 Which katakana letters are symmetrical (the same on both sides) if you draw a line through the middle from top to bottom?

Answer ほんとう (true) or うそ (a lie) after the following statements.

一 トラブル is something that's good to be in. ______

二 ライス is healthy to eat. ______

三 It's very slow driving on a ハイウエー. ______

四 You park your car in a ガレージ. ______

五 Kids hate フリータイム. ______

Unjumble the loan words and rewrite them correctly in the blank boxes provided.

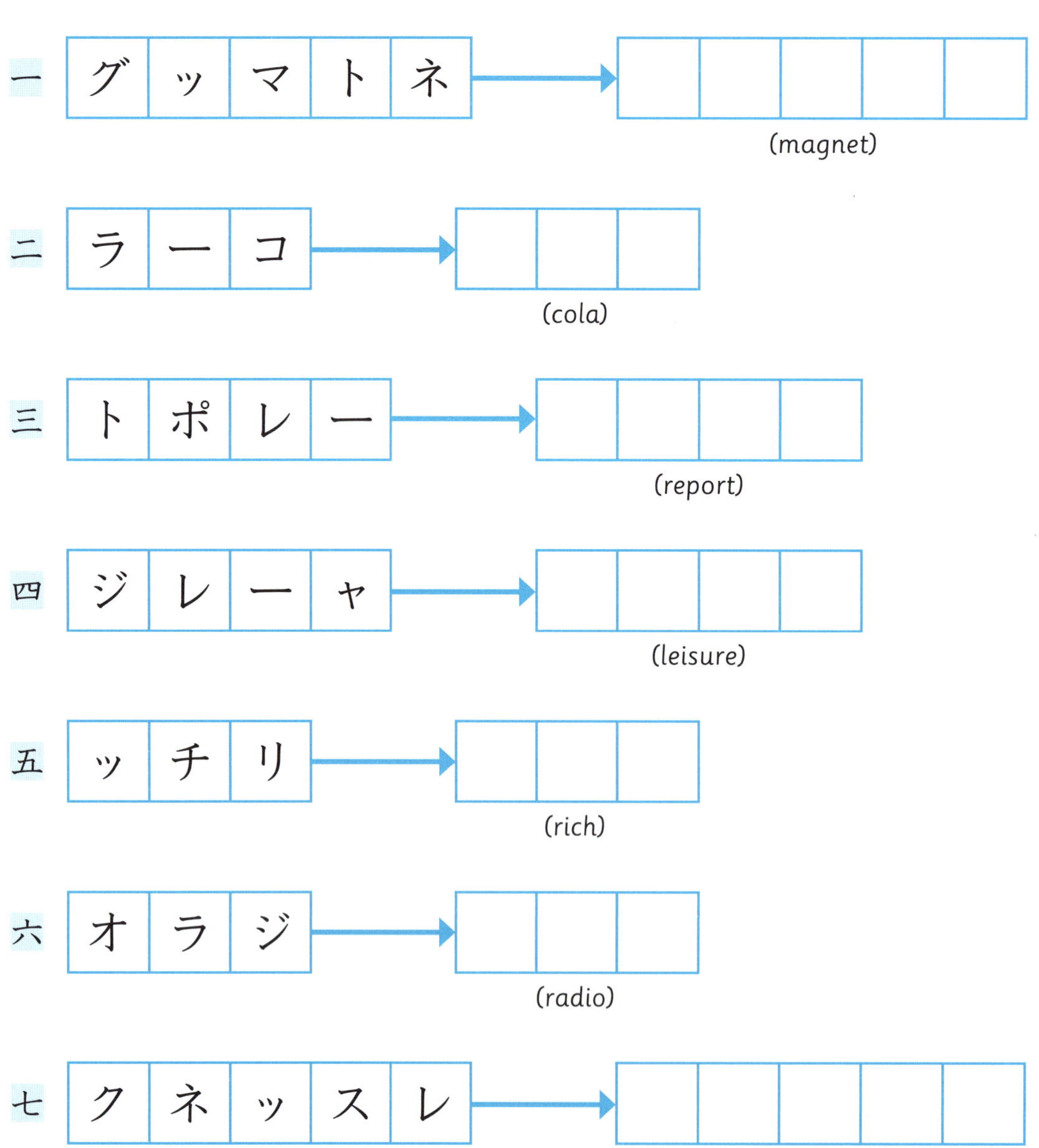

WA	'	ワ	ワ	ワ	ワ	ワ	ワ						ワ
✍													
✍													
N	`	ン	ン	ン	ン	ン	ン						ン
✍													
✍													

Change the following loan words from hiragana to katakana, then fill in the missing letters to complete the English matches.

Remember: hiragana usage is exactly the same as katakana, EXCEPT ...
the extended vowel sound is indicated with a line in katakana, rather than with another vowel, as in hiragana.

e.g. こう → コー　くう → クー
しい → シー　ねえ → ネー
さあ → サー　ふう → フー

一 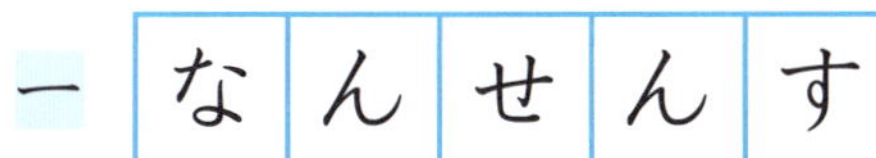

→  n _ ns _ _ s _

二 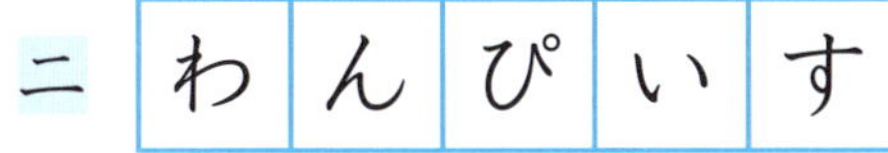

→ dr _ _ s

三 

→ w _ _ e

四 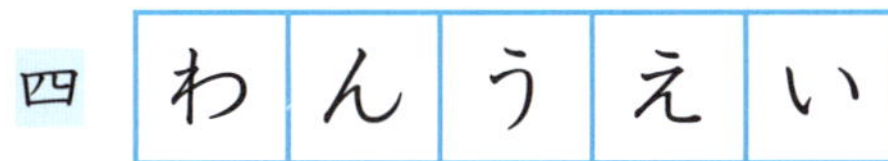

→  o _ _ w _ y

五 

→ h _ _ d _ork

CONGRATULATIONS!!!

You now know the katakana alphabet. Complete the katakana chart below to revise your letters.

A	I	U	E	O
KA	KI	KU	KE	KO
SA	SHI	SU	SE	SO
TA	CHI	TSU	TE	TO
NA	NI	NU	NE	NO
HA	HI	FU	HE	HO
MA	MI	MU	ME	MO
YA		YU		YO
RA	RI	RU	RE	RO
WA				N

GA	GI	GU	GE	GO
ZA	JI	ZU	ZE	ZO
DA			DE	DO
BA	BI	BU	BE	BO
PA	PI	PU	PE	PO

KWA	ク	ァ	ク	ァ	ク	ァ							ク	ァ
GWA	グ	ァ	グ	ァ	グ	ァ							グ	ァ
KWI	ク	ィ	ク	ィ	ク	ィ							ク	ィ
KWE	ク	ェ	ク	ェ	ク	ェ							ク	ェ
KWO	ク	ォ	ク	ォ	ク	ォ							ク	ォ

Because many sounds in non-Japanese languages cannot be written using standard katakana letters, special katakana combinations have been created to represent some of these 'foreign' sounds. These katakana combinations are only used to write loan words. Hiragana is NEVER used this way.

Connect the special katakana combination sound with the correct ending to make a loan word, then draw a line to the matching English word. The first one has been done for you.

クォー	ンチット	quarter
クェ	ツ	quintet
クォー	ター	question
クィ	スチョン	quartz

Find the loan words below in the word search, colour them in, then write them next to their English match. The first one has been done for you.

ウ	キ	ス	ポ	ー	ツ	ケ	サ	ラ	ス
イ	シ	ョ	ッ	ピ	ン	グ	テ	ジ	タ
ッ	マ	ソ	バ	チ	ェ	ラ	ツ	オ	ホ
グ	ト	ビ	デ	オ	ト	バ	ヘ	フ	ピ
コ	ン	サ	ー	ト	ナ	ス	マ	ヌ	ア
ミ	コ	ン	ピ	ュ	ー	タ	サ	ニ	ノ

一 bachelor | バ | チ | ェ | ラ |

二 concert

三 radio

四 wig

五 bus

六 sports

七 piano

八 computer

九 shopping

十 video

TI	テ	ィ	テ	ィ	テ	ィ							テ	ィ
TU	ト	ゥ	ト	ゥ	ト	ゥ							ト	ゥ
DI	デ	ィ	デ	ィ	デ	ィ							デ	ィ
YE	イ	ェ	イ	ェ	イ	ェ							イ	ェ

Fill in the missing letters to make the katakana match the English.

一 □ーティー part _

二 □エス ye _

三 ティー□エージャー t _ _ n _ ger

四 □ゥーウェー t _ o-way

五 ティー□ャツ T-sh _ _ t

六 ディス□レー dis _ lay

七 □ィナー di _ _ er

八 ディス□ウント _ iscount

九 ハ□ディー _ andy

十 □イディア ide _

Rewrite the following roomaji self introduction using hiragana and katakana letters. Make sure that all loan words are written in katakana.

hajimemashite.
watashi wa, didi desu. go sai desu.
ichi nen sei desu. aisukuriimu ga suki desu. mainichi aisukuriimu o tabemasu.
shumi wa, konpyuutageemu desu.
Konpyuuta ga daisuki desu.
supootsu wa, amari suki janai desu.
sayoonara.

Write the self introduction across the page, from left to right. Remember not to leave spaces between words!

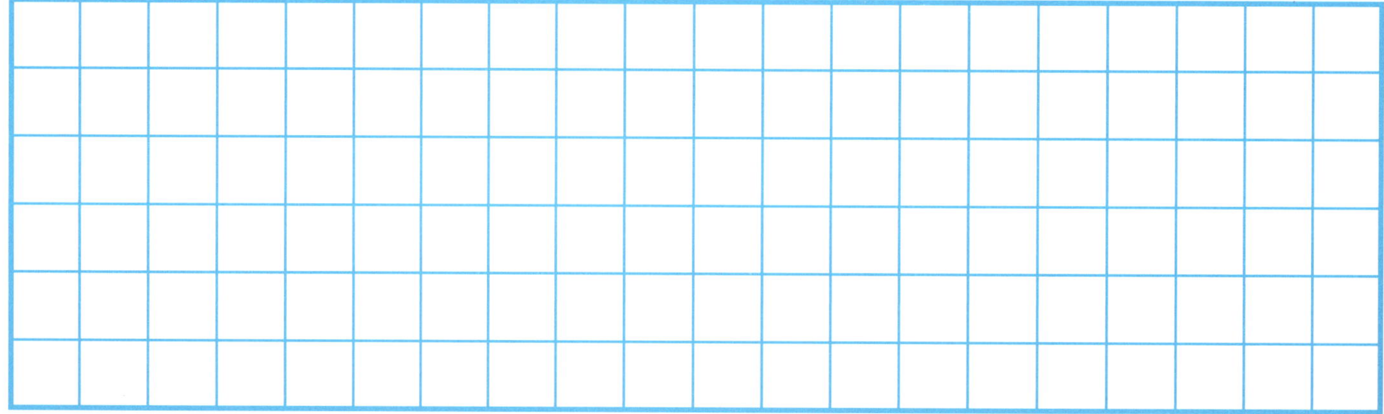

Now rewrite the self introduction in the traditional Japanese way, from right to left, and from top to bottom. Remember not to leave spaces between words!

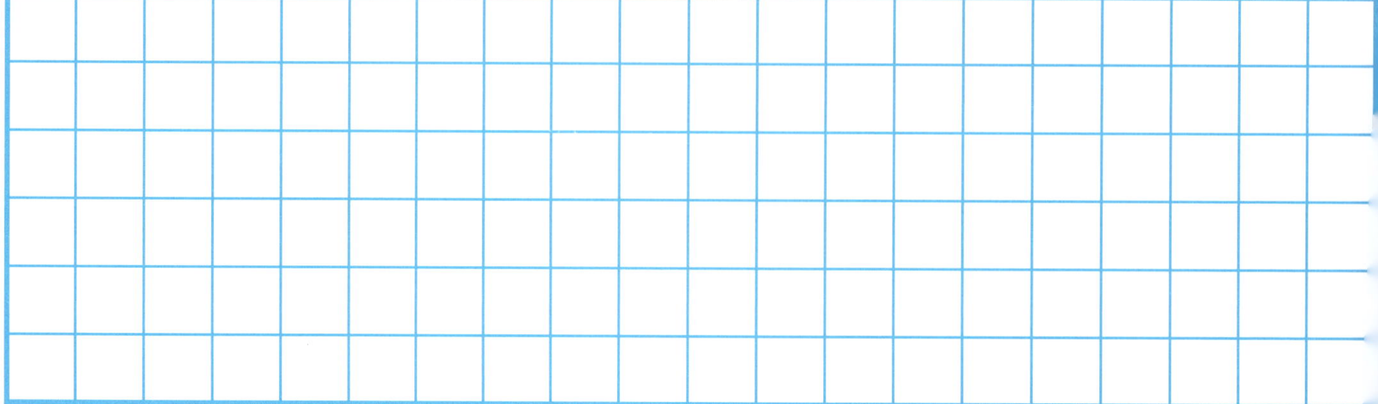

FA	フ	ァ	フ	ァ	フ	ァ							フ	ァ
FI	フ	ィ	フ	ィ	フ	ィ							フ	ィ
FYU	フ	ュ	フ	ュ	フ	ュ							フ	ュ
FE	フ	ェ	フ	ェ	フ	ェ							フ	ェ
FO	フ	ォ	フ	ォ	フ	ォ							フ	ォ

Find two matching halves of each katakana loan word, colour the two halves in the same colour, then shade the bubble with the correct English translation in the same colour. Use a different colour for each different loan word.

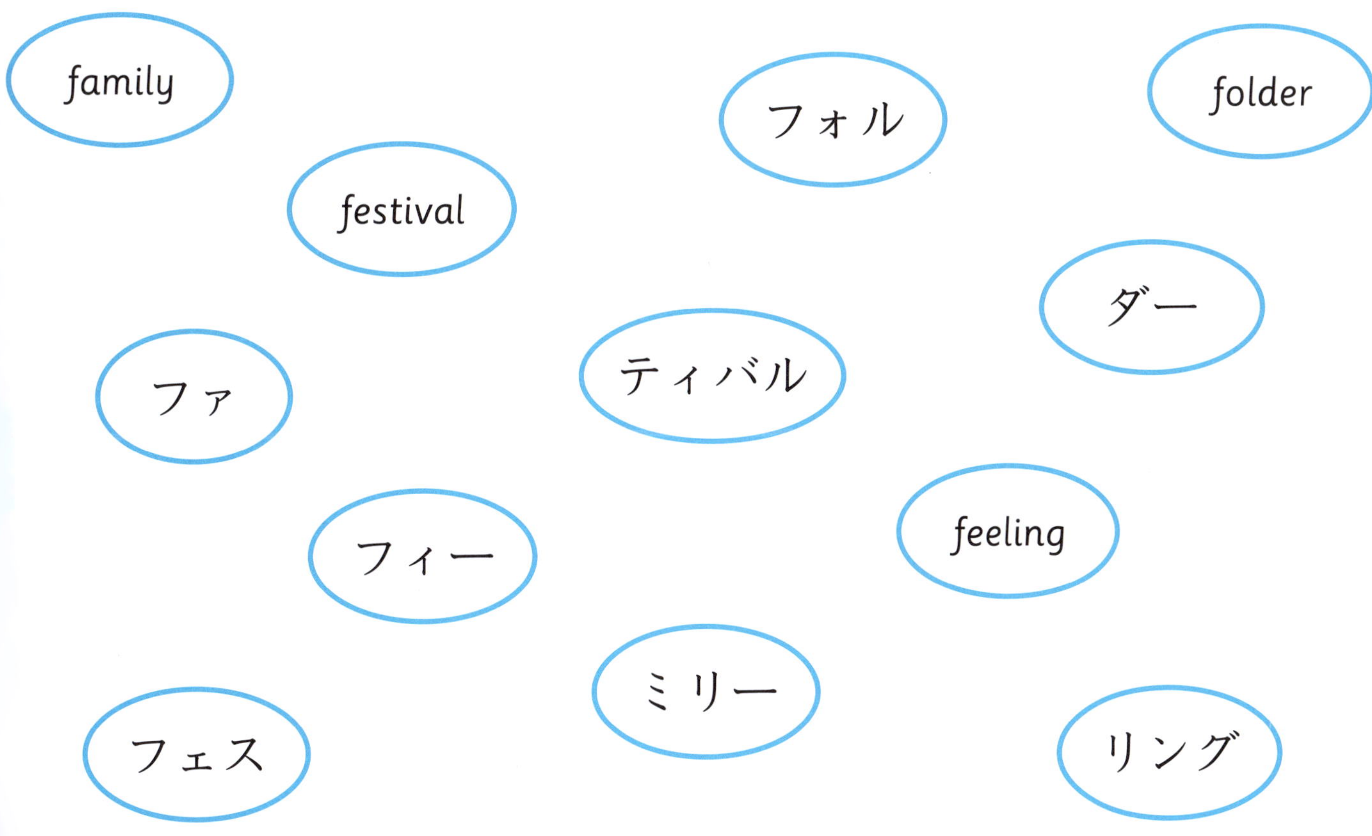

Katakana letters are not only used to write loan words, they are also used to write some special kinds of Japanese words. The most common of these is onomatopoeia – words that sound like the thing they are describing.

Using the table below as a guide, write the appropriate animal sound in the speech bubble of the animal you think makes that sound.

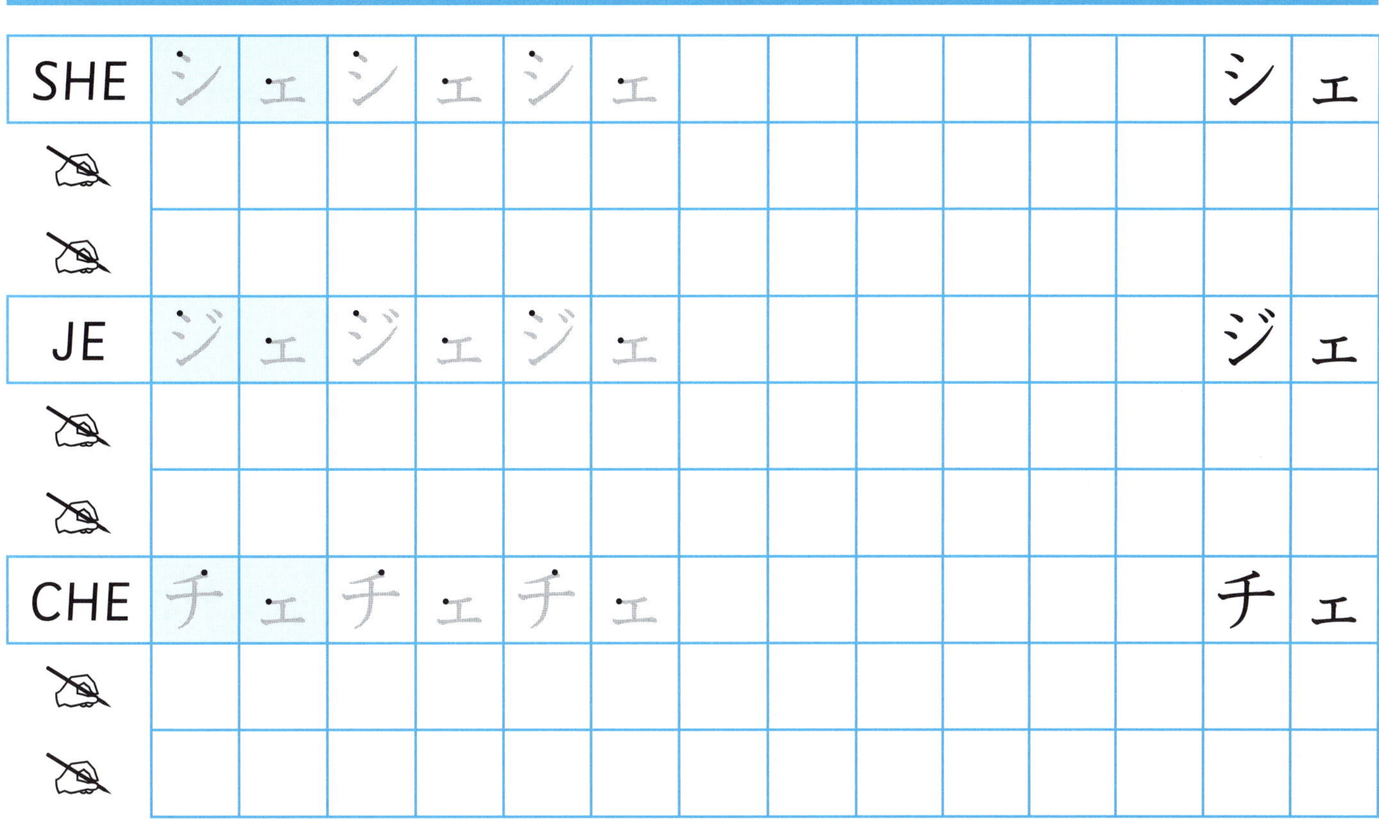

Complete each loan word by inserting one of the special katakana combinations from above, then translate your word into English.

一 ☐☐ンジ English:

二 ☐☐リー English:

三 ☐☐ット English:

四 エン☐☐ル English:

五 ☐☐ス English:

Make your way from the start of the katakana maze (スタート) to the katakana goal (ゴール). You may not pass through or around any pathways with the katakana letters or combinations beginning with K, F, or J!

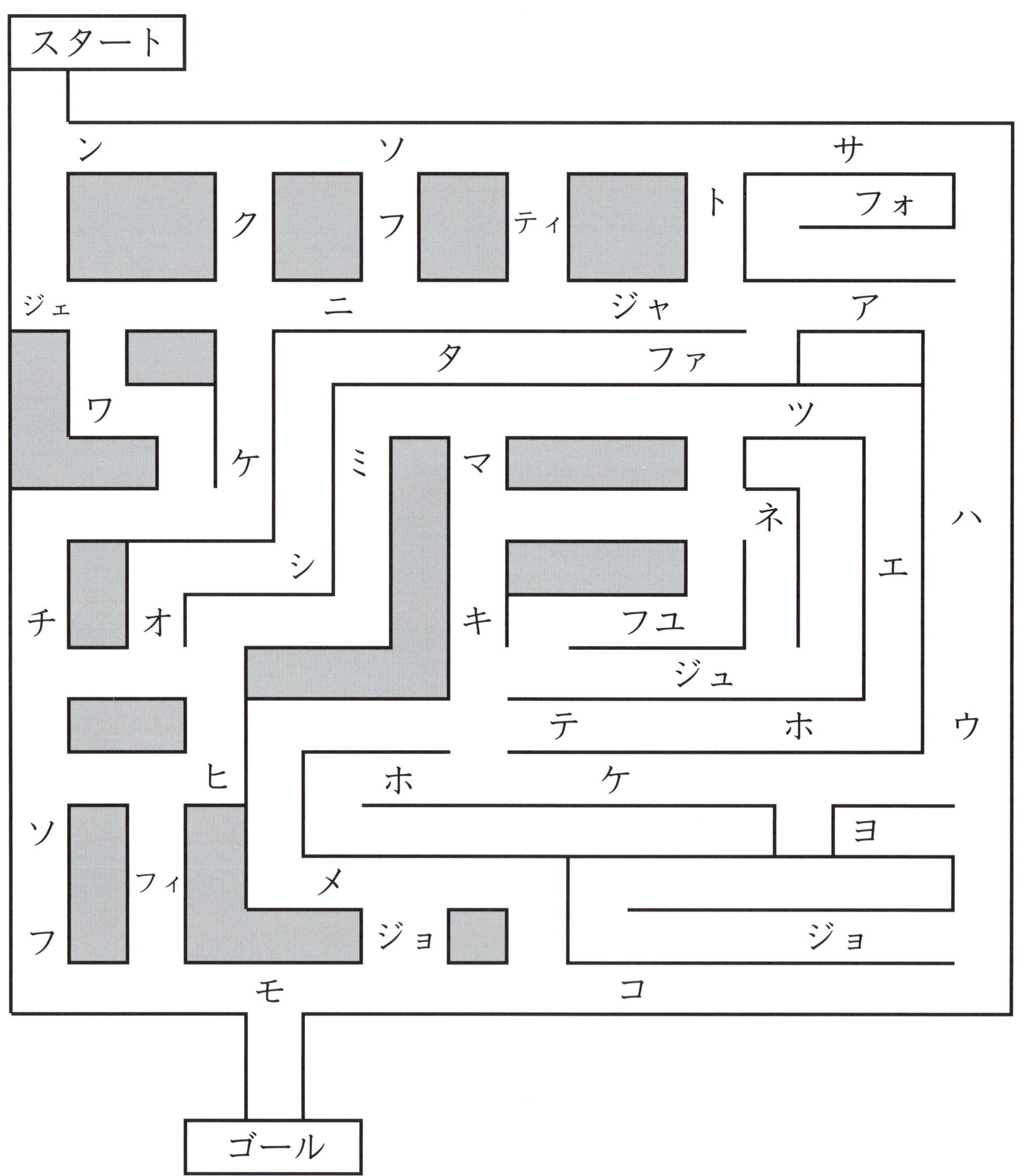

VA	ヴ	ァ	ヴ	ァ	ヴ	ァ							ヴ	ァ
✍														
VI	ヴ	ィ	ヴ	ィ	ヴ	ィ							ヴ	ィ
✍														
VU	ヴ	ヴ	ヴ	ヴ	ヴ	ヴ								ヴ
✍														
VYU	ヴ	ュ	ヴ	ュ	ヴ	ュ							ヴ	ュ
✍														
VE	ヴ	ェ	ヴ	ェ	ヴ	ェ							ヴ	ェ
✍														
VO	ヴ	ォ	ヴ	ォ	ヴ	ォ							ヴ	ォ
✍														

The English 'v' sound used to be written with a katakana 'b' sound (バビブベボ) but the special 'v' sounds listed above are now often used instead.

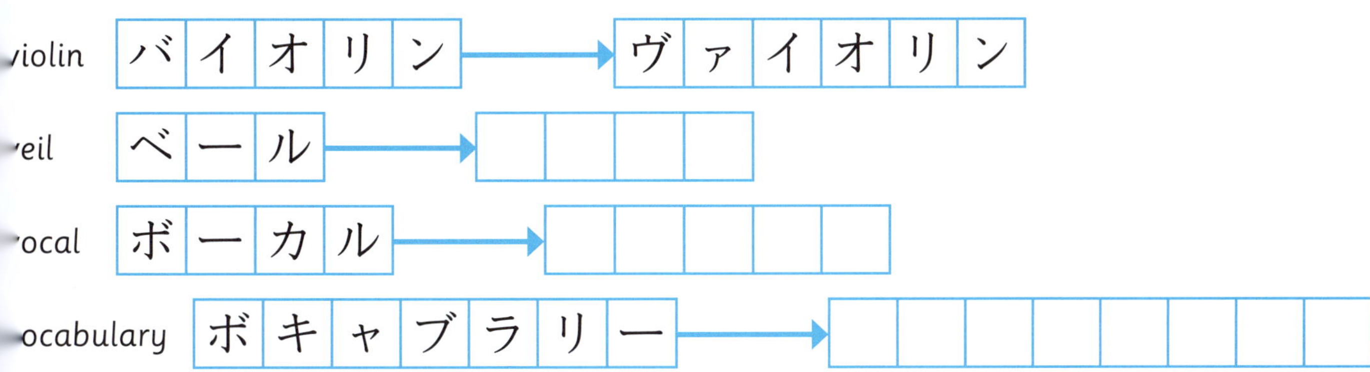

Rewrite each of the following loan words, changing the 'b' katakana letter to a 'v' katakana letter. (Both ways of spelling are correct.) The first one has been done for you.

violin バイオリン → ヴァイオリン

veil ベール → ☐☐☐☐

vocal ボーカル → ☐☐☐☐☐

vocabulary ボキャブラリー → ☐☐☐☐☐☐☐☐

Read each clue to discover the mystery object. The clues are all in English – but the English has been written using katakana letters! Read the clues and work out the mystery object.

一　ザ　ミステリー　オブジェクト　イズ　ア　ピース　オブ
クロージング。

二　ザ　ファースト　レター　イズ　ケー。

三　ザ　ラスト　レター　イズ　オー。

四　イン　ザ　オールデン　デイズ　エブリワン　ウオー　イット
イン　ジャパン。

五　ナウ　イット　イズ　オンリー　ウオーン　オン　スペシャル
オケ ーションズ。

六　ザ　サード　レター　イズ　エム。

The mystery object is a

一　ザ　ミステリー　オブジェクト　イズ　ア　マシーン。

二　ユー　カン　ユーズ　イット　フォー　ワーク　オー
プレー。

三　ザ　ラスト　レター　イズ　アール。

四　イット　ハズ　ア　キーボード。

五　イット　ハズ　ア　マウス。

The mystery object is a

WI	ウ	ィ	ウ	ィ	ウ	ィ							ウ	ィ
WE	ウ	ェ	ウ	ェ	ウ	ェ							ウ	ェ
WO	ウ	ォ	ウ	ォ	ウ	ォ							ウ	ォ

There are two ways to represent the 'w' katakana sounds. We can use the combinations above or we can use the same two katakana letters together without reducing the size of the second letter, like this:

WI → ウィ → ウイ
WE → ウェ → ウエ
WO → ウォ → ウオ

Can you recognise these words? Write the English next to each word.

一 ウィークエンド ______________________

二 ワークブック ______________________

三 ウェディング ______________________

四 ウインドー ______________________

五 ウォーター ______________________

Can you match these countries with their capital cities? Shade the matching pairs in the same colour, then join them with a line.

Choose nine items from the following list, then write one item in each bingo square. Listen to your teacher to play the game.

にほんじんです。	I'm Japanese.	しゅみ	hobby	十七	17
オーストラリアじんです。	I'm Australian.	わたしの	my (girls)	二十	20
アメリカじんです。	I'm American.	ぼくの	my (boys)	二十九	29
なにじんですか。	What nationality are you?	五ねんせい	grade 5	三十一	31
どうぞよろしく おねがいします。	a greeting used after self introduction	スポーツ	sport	三十二	32
十一さいです。	I'm 11 years old.	おんがく	music	三十六	36
しゅみはどくしょです。	My hobby is reading.	... は、あまり すきじゃないです。	I don't really like ...	四十五	45
にほんにすんでいます。	I live in Japan.	... がすきです。	I like ...	七十八	78
おげんきですか。	How are you?	... がだいすきです。	I love ...	九十三	93

LANGUAGE LESSON BINGO		

Choose nine letters, letter groups, or letter blends from the following list, then write one item in each bingo square. Listen to your teacher to play the game.

WRITING LESSON BINGO		

ア	a	コ	ko	テ	te
イ	i	サ	sa	ト	to
ウ	u	シ	shi	ガ	ga
エ	e	ス	su	ギ	gi
オ	o	セ	se	ゲ	ge
カ	ka	ソ	so	ゴ	go
キ	ki	タ	ta	ザ	za
ク	ku	チ	chi	ジ	ji
ケ	ke	ツ	tsu	ド	do

Choose nine items from the following list, then write one item in each bingo square. Listen to your teacher to play the game.

サッカーをします。	I play soccer.	クリケット	cricket	ぜんぜん	never
たかくんは、テニスをします。	Taka plays tennis.	フットボール	football	いつ	when
じゅうどうをしますか。	Do you do judo?	すいえい	swimming	どこ	where
やきゅうをしません。	I don't play baseball.	やきゅう	baseball	きょう	today
はなさんは、テニスをしません。	Hana doesn't play tennis.	げつようび	Monday	よく	often
かようびにすいえいをします。	On Tuesday I swim.	すいようび	Wednesday	あか	red
よくスポーツをします。	I often play sport.	もくようび	Thursday	あお	blue
ぜんぜんべんきょうしません。	I never study.	きんようび	Friday	しろ	white
どこでショッピングをしますか。	Where do you do shopping?	どようび	Saturday	九十七	97

LANGUAGE LESSON BINGO		

Choose nine letters, letter groups, or letter blends from the following list, then write one item in each bingo square. Listen to your teacher to play the game.

WRITING LESSON BINGO		

ヤ	ya	ヒ	hi	タ	ta
ユ	yu	フ	fu	チ	chi
ヨ	yo	ヘ	he	ツ	tsu
マ	ma	ホ	ho	テ	te
ミ	mi	ナ	na	ト	to
ム	mu	ニ	ni	シ	shi
メ	me	ヌ	nu	ケ	ke
モ	mo	ネ	ne	エ	e
ハ	ha	ノ	no	ブ	bu

Choose nine items from the following list, then write one item in each bingo square. Listen to your teacher to play the game.

いらっしゃいませ。	Welcome (to my shop).	しゅみ	hobby	十七	17
すみません。	Excuse me.	ください	please	三百二十六	326
オーストラリアじんです。	I'm Australian.	ぼくの	my (boys)	二千百十九	2119
そうですか。	Is that so?	これ	this	六百三十一	631
どうぞよろしく おねがいします。	a greeting used after self introduction	かいます	buy	五千二百三十二	5232
いくらですか。	How much is it?	ほん	book	八千三十六	8036
しゅみはどくしょです。	My hobby is reading.	... は、あまり すきじゃないです。	I don't really like ...	四百八十五	485
ありがとうございます。	Thank you very much.	まんが	cartoon, comic	七十八	78
おげんきですか。	How are you?	なに	what	九千四百四十三	9443

LANGUAGE LESSON BINGO		

Choose nine letters, letter groups, or letter blends from the following list, then write one item in each bingo square. Listen to your teacher to play the game.

WRITING LESSON BINGO		

ティ	ti	ル	ru	ギ	gi
トゥ	tu	レ	re	セ	se
イェ	ye	ロ	ro	プ	pu
グァ	gwa	ヤ	ya	カ	ka
クォ	kwo	ユ	yu	ポ	po
ワ	wa	ヨ	yo	ゾ	zo
ン	n	マ	ma	ウ	u
ラ	ra	メ	me	ア	a
リ	ri	モ	mo	ザ	za

Choose nine items from the following list, then write one item in each bingo square. Listen to your teacher to play the game.

たのしかったです。	It was fun.	だれ	who	うち	home
にほんごは、たのしいです。	Japanese is fun.	なに	what	ほん	book
ピピちゃんは、かわいいです。	Pipi is cute.	どこ	where	うみ	beach
どうでしたか。	How was it?	おかあさん	mother	で	at
ほんをかいました。	I bought a book.	がっこう	school	か	?
おげんきですか。	How are you?	みせ	shop(s)	三百四十五	345
すみません。	Excuse me.	としょかん	library	二千十六	2016
よくスポーツをします。	I often play sport.	しました	I did	八千	8000
ともだちと	with a friend	のみました	I drank	六百五十三	653

LANGUAGE LESSON BINGO		

Choose nine letters, letter groups, or letter blends from the following list, then write one item in each bingo square. Listen to your teacher to play the game.

WRITING LESSON BINGO		

ウィ	wi	ウェ	we	ウォ	wo
ユ	yu	フ	fu	チ	chi
ヴァ	va	ヴ	vu	ヴェ	ve
マ	ma	ホ	ho	テ	te
ヴュ	vyu	ヴォ	vo	ヴィ	vi
ム	mu	ニ	ni	シ	shi
シェ	she	ジェ	je	チェ	che
モ	mo	ネ	ne	エ	e
ファ	fa	フィ	fi	フォ	fo

LISTENING

Listen to the teacher, then circle the correct answer.

1	2	3	4	5
American (person) Japanese (person) New Zealander	12 years old grade 12 12	hobby reading music	My name is Yumi. I'm pleased to meet you. Where do you live?	How are you? How old are you? What grade are you in?

6	7	8	9	10
How old are you? I'm pleased to meet you. What's your hobby?	I'm in grade 5. I'm 5 years old. My hobby is music.	shopping computer games sport	I love Japan. I live in Japan. I like Japan.	I don't really like sport. My hobby is sport. Do you like sport?

READING

Look at the cards the teacher will show you. Circle the correct answer.

1	2	3	4	5
E SE TA	U O SU	CHI SO I	DE KA TE	GU KE GE

6	7	8	9	10
KO SO GA	ZE DO TO	SHI JI TO	A KU ZA	U KA GA

CONGRATULATIONS! You remembered  things about Japan and its language.

HOW MUCH CAN YOU REMEMBER? LL 1 – 10; WL 1 – 8

LISTENING

Listen to the teacher, then circle the correct answer.

1	2	3	4	5
soccer cricket basketball	I play. Do you play? I do not play.	when often today	Monday Wednesday Sunday	what kind of swimming baseball

6	7	8	9	10
park where shop(s)	I study at school. I like study. I do not study.	Tuesday home sometimes	library swimming reading	I like swimming. I don't swim at all. I often swim.

READING

Look at the cards the teacher will show you. Circle the correct answer.

1	2	3	4	5
YA A HI	E MO ME	HO FU GO	TSU SO SHI	MO MI ME

6	7	8	9	10
BA MU MA	NA TO HO	NO NE ME	PU KE KU	JI CHI TSU

CONGRATULATIONS! You remembered ______ things about Japan and its language.

HOW MUCH CAN YOU REMEMBER? LL 1 – 15; WL 1 – 12

LISTENING

Listen to the teacher, then circle the correct answer.

1	2	3	4	5
video game song computer game	tomorrow sometimes not at all	cartoon book 2000	What will you buy? I do not buy books. Books are boring.	How are you? This is good. Is that so?

6	7	8	9	10
Excuse me, but … How much is it? What's your hobby?	Yes it is, isn't it? enjoyable/ fun cute	interesting small today	May I have this, please? It is big, isn't it? My hobby is reading.	I don't really like cartoons. My hobby is cartoons. Cartoons are interesting.

READING

Look at the cards the teacher will show you. Circle the correct answer.

1	2	3	4	5
E FU HE	U O CHI	HI SO I	DE GA TE	WA KE N

6	7	8	9	10
KO RO RU	ZE YU RE	BA JI TO	KWO YE DI	KWE YE TI

CONGRATULATIONS! You remembered ______ things about Japan and its language.

LISTENING

Listen to the teacher, then circle the correct answer.

1	2	3	4	5
sports field department store sport	library beach school	friend mother father	I went to school. I ate at home. Where did you read?	I drink juice. I like juice. I drank juice.

6	7	8	9	10
TV what shop(s)	It was fun. It is fun. It was boring.	How was it? How are you? How old are you?	I read a book. I studied. I ate with a friend.	Japanese is good. Do you learn Japanese? Where do you learn Japanese?

READING

Look at the cards the teacher will show you. Circle the correct answer.

1	2	3	4	5
YA A ME	E TA ME	SO RU RA	TSU SO SHI	WA U RA

6	7	8	9	10
WO VO TI	VA WI DI	VE VYU JI	JE SHE KWA	FYU FO FI

CONGRATULATIONS! You remembered ______ things about Japan and its language.

WORDLIST

WORDLIST – ENGLISH/JAPANESE	
ENGLISH	JAPANESE/ROOMAJI
1 · one	一 / いち I CHI
1 o'clock	一じ / いちじ I CHI JI
10 · ten	十 / じゅう JU U
10 o'clock	十じ / じゅうじ JU U JI
100 · one hundred	百 / ひゃく HYA KU
1000	千 / 一千 / せん / いっせん SE N / I S SE N
11 · eleven	十一 / じゅう いち JU U I CHI
11 o'clock	十一じ / じゅういちじ JU U I CHI JI
12 · twelve	十二 / じゅう に JU U NI
12 o'clock	十二じ / じゅうにじ JU U NI JI
13 · thirteen	十三 / じゅう さん JU U SA N
14 · fourteen	十四 / じゅう し / よん JU U SHI / YO N
15 · fifteen	十五 / じゅう ご JU U GO
16 · sixteen	十六 / じゅう ろく JU U RO KU
17 · seventeen	十七 / じゅう しち / なな JU U SHI CHI / NA NA
18 · eighteen	十八 / じゅう はち JU U HA CHI
19 · nineteen	十九 / じゅう く / きゅう JU U KU / KYU U
2 · two	二 / に NI
2 o'clock	二じ / にじ NI JI
20 · twenty	二十 / にじゅう NI JU U
200	二百 / にひゃく NI HYA KU
2000	二千 / にせん NI SE N
21 · twenty-one	二十一 / にじゅういち NI JU U I CHI
3 · three	三 / さん SA N
3 o'clock	三じ / さんじ SA N JI
30 · thirty	三十 / さんじゅう SA N JU U
300	三百 / さんびゃく SA N BYA KU
3000	三千 / さんぜん SA N ZE N
4 · four	四 / し / よん SHI / YO N
4 o'clock	四じ / よじ YO JI
40 · forty	四十 / よんじゅう YO N JU U
400	四百 / よんひゃく YO N HYA KU
4000	四千 / よんせん YO N SE N
5 · five	五 / ご GO
5 o'clock	五じ / ごじ GO JI
50 · fifty	五十 / ご じゅう GO JU U
500	五百 / ごひゃく GO HYA KU
5000	五千 / ごせん GO SE N
6 · six	六 / ろく RO KU

WORDLIST – ENGLISH/JAPANESE	
ENGLISH	JAPANESE/ROOMAJI
6 o'clock	六じ / ろくじ RO KU JI
60 · sixty	六十 / ろくじゅう RO KU JU U
600	六百 / ろっぴゃく RO P PYA KU
6000	六千 / ろくせん RO KU SE N
7 · seven	七 / しち / なな SHI CHI / NA NA
7 o'clock	七じ / しちじ SHI CHI JI
70 · seventy	七十 / しち / なな じゅう SHI CHI / NA NA JU U
700	七百 / ななひゃく NA NA HYA KU
7000	七千 / ななせん NA NA SE N
8 · eight	八 / はち HA CHI
8 o'clock	八じ / はちじ HA CHI JI
80 · eighty	八十 / はちじゅう HA CHI JU U
800	八百 / はっぴゃく HA P PYA KU
8000	八千 / はっせん HA S SE N
9 · nine	九 / く / きゅう KU / KYU U
9 o'clock	九じ / くじ KU JI
90 · ninety	九十 / きゅうじゅう KYU U JU U
900	九百 / きゅうひゃく KYU U HYA KU
9000	九千 / きゅうせん KYU U SE N
Africa	アフリカ A FU RI KA
am/is/are	です DE SU
America	アメリカ A ME RI KA
American (person)	アメリカじん A ME RI KA JI N
and	と TO
and also/then	そして SO SHI TE
April	四がつ / しがつ SHI GA TSU
Asia	アジア A JI A
at (a time)	に NI
ate	たべました TA BE MA SHI TA
August	八がつ / はちがつ HA CHI GA TSU
Australia	オーストラリア O O SU TO RA RI A
Australian (person)	オーストラリアじん O O SU TO RA RI A JI N
autumn	あき A KI
baseball	やきゅう YA KYU U
basketball	バスケットボール BA SU KE T TO BO O RU
beach/sea	うみ U MI
bicycle	じてんしゃ JI TE N SHA
big	おおきい O O KI I
(my) birthday	たんじょうび TA N JO O BI

WORDLIST – ENGLISH/JAPANESE	
ENGLISH	JAPANESE/ROOMAJI
(your) birthday	おたんじょうび O TA N YO O BI
black	くろ KU RO
blue	あお A O
book	ほん HO N
boring	つまらない TSU MA RA NA I
bought	かいました KA I MA SHI TA
brother (older)	おにいさん O NI I SA N
brother (younger)	おとうと O TO O TO
brown	ちゃいろ CHA I RO
bus	バス BA SU
buy	かいます KA I MA SU
by (transport)	で DE
Canada	カナダ KA NA DA
Canadian (person)	カナダじん KA NA DA JI N
car	くるま KU RU MA
cartoon, comic	まんが MA N GA
China	ちゅうごく CHU U GO KU
Chinese (person)	ちゅうごくじん CHU U GO KU JI N
cinema	えいがかん E I GA KA N
coffee	コーヒー KO O HI I
cold	さむい SA MU I
computer games	コンピュータゲーム KO N PYU U TA GE E MU
cool	すずしい SU ZU SHI I
cricket	クリケット KU RI KE T TO
December	十二がつ / じゅうにがつ JU U NI GA TSU
department store	デパート DE PA A TO
did	しました SHI MA SHI TA
didn't go	いきませんでした I KI MA SE N DE SHI TA
do not go	いきません I KI MA SE N
do/play	します SHI MA SU
don't buy	かいません KA I MA SE N
don't play/do	しません SHI MA SE N
drank	のみました NO MI MA SHI TA
drink	のみます NO MI MA SU
eat	たべます TA BE MA SU
England	イギリス I GI RI SU
English (person)	イギリスじん I GI RI SU JI N
Europe	ヨーロッパ YO O RO P PA
every day	まいにち MA I NI CHI
Excuse me, but …	すみませんが、… SU MI MA SE N GA
Excuse me.	すみません。 SU MI MA SE N
eye(s)	め ME

WORDLIST – ENGLISH/JAPANESE	
ENGLISH	JAPANESE/ROOMAJI
father	おとうさん O TO O SA N
February	二がつ / にがつ NI GA TSU
football	フットボール FU T TO BO O RU
Friday	きんようび KI N YO O BI
fried noodles	やきそば YA KI SO BA
friend	ともだち TO MO DA CHI
fun/enjoyable	たのしい TA NO SHI I
go	いきます I KI MA SU
good	いい I I
grade	ねんせい NE N SE I
green tea	おちゃ O CHA
greeting used after introducing oneself	どおぞ よろしく DO O ZO YO RO SHI KU （おねがいします） O NE GA I SHI MA SU
hair	かみのけ KA MI NO KE
hamburger	ハンバーガー HA N BA A GA A
hello (good day)	こんにちは KO N NI CHI WA
Here you are.	どうぞ。 DO O ZO
hobby	しゅみ SHU MI
Hokkaido	ほっかいどう HO K KA I DO O
home	うち U CHI
Honshu	ほんしゅう HO N SHU U
hot	あつい A TSU I
hot dog	ホットドッグ HO T TO DO G GU
how much	いくら I KU RA
I (used by boys)	ぼく BO KU
I (used mostly by girls)	わたし WA TA SHI
I'm pleased to meet you.	はじめまして。 HA JI ME MA SHI TE
ice-cream	アイスクリーム A I SU KU RI I MU
in (a season)	に NI
interesting/funny	おもしろい O MO SHI RO I
isn't it?	ね NE
January	一がつ / いちがつ I CHI GA TSU
Japan	にほん / にっぽん NI HO N / NI P PO N
Japanese (language)	にほんご NI HO N GO
Japanese (person)	にほんじん NI HO N JI N
juice	ジュース JU U SU
Judo	じゅうどう JU U DO O
July	七がつ / しちがつ SHI CHI GA TSU
June	六がつ / ろくがつ RO KU GA TSU
Kyushu	きゅうしゅう KYU U SHU U
library	としょかん TO SHO KA N
like	すき SU KI

WORDLIST – ENGLISH/JAPANESE	
ENGLISH	JAPANESE/ROOMAJI
March	三がつ / さんがつ SA N GA TSU
May	五がつ / ごがつ GO GA TSU
milk	ミルク MI RU KU
Monday	げつようび GE TSU YO O BI
mother	おかあさん O KA A SA N
music	おんがく O N GA KU
my (for boys)	ぼくの BO KU NO
my (for girls)	わたしの WA TA SHI NO
(my) name	なまえ NA MA E
(your) name	おなまえ O NA MA E
New Zealand	ニュージーランド NYU U JI I RA N DO
New Zealander	ニュージーランドじん NYU U JI I RA N DO JI N
no	いいえ I I E
North America	きた アメリカ KI TA A ME RI KA
not at all	ぜんぜん ZE N ZE N
November	十一がつ / じゅう いちがつ JU U I CHI GA TSU
October	十がつ / じゅうがつ JU U GA TSU
often	よく YO KU
on (a day)	に NI
Osaka	おおさか O O SA KA
... person	... じん JI N
pants	ズボン ZU BO N
park	こうえん KO O E N
particle wa	は WA
pizza	ピザ PI ZA
plane	ひこうき HI KO O KI
play/do	します SHI MA SU
played/did	しました SHI MA SHI TA
please	ください KU DA SA I
Please be quiet.	しずかにしてください。 SHI ZU KA NI SHI TE KU DA SA I
ease close your book.	ほんをとじてください。 HO N O TO JI TE KU DA SA I
Please listen.	きいてください。 KI I TE KU DA SA I
Please look.	みてください。 MI TE KU DA SA I
ease open your book.	ほんをひらいてください。 HO N O HI RA I TE KU DA SA I
Please sit.	すわってください。 SU WA T TE KU DA SA I
Please stand.	たってください。 TA T TE KU DA SA I
question particle	か KA
read	よみます YO MI MA SU
read (past tense)	よみました YO MI MA SHI TA
reading (the hobby)	どくしょ DO KU SHO
red	あか A KA
Russia	ロシア RO SHI A

WORDLIST – ENGLISH/JAPANESE	
ENGLISH	JAPANESE/ROOMAJI
Russian (person)	ロシアじん RO SHI A JI N
said after eating	ごちそうさまでした。 GO CHI SO O SA MA DE SHI TA
said before eating	いただきます。 I TA DA KI MA SU
sandwich	サンドイッチ SA N DO I T CHI
Saturday	どようび DO YO O BI
saw/watched	みました MI MA SHI TA
school	がっこう GA K KO O
sea/beach	うみ U MI
see/watch	みます MI MA SU
September	九がつ / くがつ KU GA TSU
Shikoku	しこく SHI KO KU
shirt	シャツ SHA TSU
shoes	くつ KU TSU
shop(s)	みせ MI SE
shopping	ショッピング SHO P PI N GU
sister (older)	おねえさん O NE E SA N
sister (younger)	いもうと I MO O TO
small	ちいさい CHI I SA I
soccer	サッカー SA K KA A
socks	くつした KU TSU SHI TA
sometimes	ときどき TO KI DO KI
song	うた U TA
South America	みなみ アメリカ MI NA MI A ME RI KA
sport	スポーツ SU PO O TSU
sports field	グランド GU RA N DO
spring	はる HA RU
studied/learnt	べんきょう しました BE N KYO O SHI MA SHI TA
study/learn	べんきょう します BE N KYO O SHI MA SU
summer	なつ NA TSU
Sunday	にちようび NI CHI YO O BI
swimming	すいえい SU I E I
TV	テレビ TE RE BI
tea (green)	おちゃ O CHA
teacher	せんせい SE N SE I
tennis	テニス TE NI SU
thank you very much	ありがとうございます A RI GA TO O GO ZA I MA SU
Thank you for the food. (said after eating)	ごちそうさまでした。 GO CHI SO O SA MA DE SHI TA
that	それ SO RE
that (over there)	あれ A RE
this	これ KO RE
this year	ことし KO TO SHI
Thursday	もくようび MO KU YO O BI

WORDLIST – ENGLISH/JAPANESE	
ENGLISH	JAPANESE/ROOMAJI
to (a place)	に NI
today	きょう KYO O
Tokyo	とうきょう TO O KYO O
tomorrow	あした A SHI TA
Tuesday	かようび KA YO O BI
used after boy's name	くん KU N
used after girl's name	さん SA N
video game	テレビゲーム TE RE BI GE E MU
warm	あたたかい A TA TA KA I
was big	おおきかったです O O KI KA T TA DE SU
was boring	つまらなかったです TSU MA RA NA KA T TA DE SU
was cute	かわいかったです KA WA I KA T TA DE SU
was fun/enjoyable	たのしかったです TA NO SHI KA T TA DE SU
was good	よかったです YO KA T TA DE SU
was interesting/funny	おもしろかったです O MO SHI RO KA T TA DE SU
was small	ちいさかったです CHI I SA KA T TA DE SU
water	みず MI ZU

WORDLIST – ENGLISH/JAPANESE	
ENGLISH	JAPANESE/ROOMAJI
water monster	かっぱ KA P PA
Wednesday	すいようび SU I YO O BI
Welcome (to my shop).	いらっしゃいませ。 I RA S SHA I MA SE
went	いきました I KI MA SHI TA
what	なに / なん NA NI / NA N
what kind of	どんな DO N NA
what month	なんがつ NA N GA TSU
what nationality	なにじん NA NI JI N
when	いつ I TSU
where	どこ DO KO
who	だれ DA RE
winter	ふゆ FU YU
years old	さいです SA I DE SU
yellow	きいろ KI I RO
yen	えん E N
yes	はい HA I
zoo	どうぶつえん DO O BU TSU E N

SENTENCE PATTERN LIST

SENTENCE PATTERN LIST – ENGLISH/JAPANESE	
ENGLISH	JAPANESE/ROOMAJI
☺A☺ is ☺B☺	☺A☺ は、☺B☺ です。 WA, DE SU.
How are you?	おげんきですか。 O GE N KI DE SU KA?
How much is it?	いくらですか。 I KU RA DE SU KA?
I am ☺☺☺ years old.	☺☺☺ さい です。 SA I DE SU.
I am in grade ☺☺☺.	☺☺☺ ねんせいです。 NE N SE I DE SU.
I am ☺name☺.	☺name☺です。 DE SU.
I am ☺nationality☺.	☺country☺じんです。 JI N DE SU.
I don't really like ☺☺☺.	☺☺☺ は、あまり WA, A MA RI すきじゃないです。 SU KI JA NA I DE SU
I go to ☺☺☺.	☺☺☺ にいきます。 NI I KI MA SU.
I like ☺☺☺.	☺☺☺ が すき です。 GA SU KI DE SU.
I live in ☺☺☺.	☺☺☺ にすんでいます。 NI SU N DE I MA SU.
I love ☺☺☺.	☺☺☺ がだいすきです。 GA DA I SU KI DE SU.
I'm fine. (Yes, I'm well.)	(はい) げんきです。 HA I GE N KI DE SU.
I play/do ☺activity☺.	☺activity☺をします。 O SHI MA SU.

SENTENCE PATTERN LIST – ENGLISH/JAPANESE	
ENGLISH	JAPANESE/ROOMAJI
Is that so?	そうですか。 SO O DE SU KA?
It's ☺☺☺ yen.	☺☺☺ えんです。 E N DE SU.
May I have ☺☺☺?	☺☺☺ をください。 O KU DA SA I?
My hobby is ☺☺☺.	しゅみは、☺☺☺ です。 SHU MI WA, DE SU.
This is a ☺☺☺.	これは、☺☺☺ です。 KO RE WA, DE SU.
What did (you) do?	なにをしましたか。 NA NI O SHI MA SHI TA KA?
What is it like?	どうですか。 DO O DE SU KA?
What is this?	これは、なんですか。 KO RE WA, NA N DE SU KA?
What is your hobby?	しゅみは、なんですか。 SHU MI WA, NA N DE SU KA?
What kind of sport do you play?	どんなスポーツをしますか。 DO N NA SU PO O TSU O SHI MA SU KA?
What nationality are you?	なにじんですか。 NA NI JI N DE SU KA?
What was it like?	どうでしたか。 DO O DE SHI TA KA?
Where will you go?	どこにいきますか。 DO KO NI I KI MA SU KA?
Yes it is, isn't it?	そうですね。 SO O DE SU NE?

あ A	い I	う U	え E	お O
か KA	き KI	く KU	け KE	こ KO
が GA	ぎ GI	ぐ GU	げ GE	ご GO
さ SA	し SHI	す SU	せ SE	そ SO
ざ ZA	じ JI	ず ZU	ぜ ZE	ぞ ZO
た TA	ち CHI	つ TSU	て TE	と TO
だ DA			で DE	ど DO
な NA	に NI	ぬ NU	ね NE	の NO
は HA	ひ HI	ふ FU	へ HE	ほ HO
ば BA	び BI	ぶ BU	べ BE	ぼ BO
ぱ PA	ぴ PI	ぷ PU	ぺ PE	ぽ PO
ま MA	み MI	む MU	め ME	も MO
や YA		ゆ YU		よ YO
ら RA	り RI	る RU	れ RE	ろ RO
わ WA				を particle O
ん N				

HIRAGANA COMBINATION CHART

きゃ	きゅ	きょ
kya	kyu	kyo
ぎゃ	ぎゅ	ぎょ
gya	gyu	gyo
しゃ	しゅ	しょ
sha	shu	sho
じゃ	じゅ	じょ
ja	ju	jo
ちゃ	ちゅ	ちょ
cha	chu	cho
にゃ	にゅ	にょ
nya	nyu	nyo
ひゃ	ひゅ	ひょ
hya	hyu	hyo
びゃ	びゅ	びょ
bya	byu	byo
ぴゃ	ぴゅ	ぴょ
pya	pyu	pyo
みゃ	みゅ	みょ
mya	myu	myo
りゃ	りゅ	りょ
rya	ryu	ryo

ア A	イ I	ウ U	エ E	オ O
カ KA	キ KI	ク KU	ケ KE	コ KO
ガ GA	ギ GI	グ GU	ゲ GE	ゴ GO
サ SA	シ SHI	ス SU	セ SE	ソ SO
ザ ZA	ジ JI	ズ ZU	ゼ ZE	ゾ ZO
タ TA	チ CHI	ツ TSU	テ TE	ト TO
ダ DA			デ DE	ド DO
ナ NA	ニ NI	ヌ NU	ネ NE	ノ NO
ハ HA	ヒ HI	フ FU	ヘ HE	ホ HO
バ BA	ビ BI	ブ BU	ベ BE	ボ BO
パ PA	ピ PI	プ PU	ペ PE	ポ PO
マ MA	ミ MI	ム MU	メ ME	モ MO
ヤ YA		ユ YU		ヨ YO
ラ RA	リ RI	ル RU	レ RE	ロ RO
ワ WA				ン N

KATAKANA COMBINATION CHART

キャ	キュ	キョ
kya	kyu	kyo
ギャ	ギュ	ギョ
gya	gyu	gyo
シャ	シュ	ショ
sha	shu	sho
ジャ	ジュ	ジョ
ja	ju	jo
チャ	チュ	チョ
cha	chu	cho
ニャ	ニュ	ニョ
nya	nyu	nyo
ヒャ	ヒュ	ヒョ
hya	hyu	hyo
ビャ	ビュ	ビョ
bya	byu	byo
ピャ	ピュ	ピョ
pya	pyu	pyo
ミャ	ミュ	ミョ
mya	myu	myo
リャ	リュ	リョ
rya	ryu	ryo

クァ	グァ	クィ	クェ	クォ
kwa	gwa	kwi	kwe	kwo
ティ	トゥ	ディ	ウェ	
ti	tu	di	ye	
ファ	フィ	フュ	フェ	フォ
fa	fi	fyu	fe	fo
シェ	ジェ	チェ		ヴォ
she	je	che		vo
ヴァ	ヴィ	ヴ	ヴュ	ヴェ
va	vi	vu	vyu	ve
ウィ	ウェ	ウォ		
wi	we	wo		